Grades 6–7

Toolkit Texts

Selected by **Stephanie Harvey & Anne Goudvis**

Short Nonfiction for Guided and Independent Practice

Correlated to

The Comprehension Toolkit

From our perspective, we can never have enough short text. It is accessible, to the point, and in a word—short! *Toolkit Texts* is designed to capture kids' interest, engage them in real-world reading, and give them time to just plain read! The real world is rich, fascinating, and compelling and kids love to explore it through reading. We hope these short nonfiction articles will bring a bit of that outside world into your classrooms. Enjoy!

Stephanie Harvey   Anne Goudvis

Toolkit Texts Grades 6–7

Table of Contents

Introduction

Reading, writing, talking, listening, and investigating are the hallmarks of active literacy. Throughout the school day and across the curriculum, kids are actively questioning, inferring, discussing, debating, inquiring, and generating new ideas. An active literacy classroom fairly bursts with joyful, enthusiastic learning.

This kind of literacy requires tons of great text for kids to read. *Toolkit Texts* is a compilation of engaging nonfiction articles, in both English and Spanish, on a variety of topics and at a range of reading levels. If you are currently using *The Comprehension Toolkit*, you already have an extensive amount of text at your fingertips. *Toolkit Texts* will give you even more. Additionally, you can use these short text articles in *any* of your literacy and content instruction, for science reading, for social studies reading, and as models for nonfiction writing across the curriculum.

Nonfiction is potentially the most accessible genre. You don't even have to read the words to get information from it. The photographs, illustrations, maps, and other features hook kids and reel them in. Nonfiction varies in quality, however, so we have searched long and hard to find the very best texts to include in this resource. We were delighted to discover that the Carus family of children's magazines—*Appleseeds, Ask, Click, Cobblestone, Odyssey*, and *Faces*—provided just what we were looking for.

We are pleased to offer both English and Spanish versions of every article in this volume on the enclosed CD-ROM. After the translations were completed, they were reviewed by bilingual teachers who read them with their students in mind. You can search the CD-ROM for an article by topic or by comprehension strategy, then print out either the English or Spanish version.

"The children are the future . . ."
—Femke Oldham

The banner, which traveled thousands of miles, is held up by Majiwa students.

In fact, educating girls may be the smartest way to bring families out of poverty. Girls who have been to school are more likely to have smaller families, and healthier, better-educated children. The benefits of this education range from being able to read instructions on pill bottles, to making better decisions, to getting a job.

Most countries are committed to making sure all children get some education. Recently, Kenya made primary school free again. Girls who want to go to high school, however, must attend costly boarding schools. On Vashon Island, the bake sales continue; middle school students are selling hacky sacks to help out, too.

Emma Bean shared the dream of her fellow students: "We're hoping that by helping one part of the village, we can help the whole community."

"The children are the future," added Femke Oldham. "We're giving them the opportunity to have a good future with lots of options."

Adapted from an article by Lesley Reed

39

"Los niños son el futuro . . ."
—Femke Oldham

Esta pancarta, que viajó miles de millas, está sostenida por los estudiantes de Majiwa.

El Club Interactivo también decidió pagar los gastos escolares de Gideon, Carolina, Jacqueline, y Benjamín. Para realizarlo, llevan a cabo escuela de pasteles y venden dulces. En particular, desean asegurar que Jacqueline y Carolina continúen sus estudios porque para las niñas, asistir a la escuela reduce a la mitad el riesgo de contraer el SIDA. Al fin de cuentas, la educación no sólo es importante para desarrollar las aptitudes—es su mejor esperanza para la vida en sí.

De hecho, educar a las niñas puede ser la manera más inteligente de hacer que las familias salgan de la pobreza. Las niñas que han asistido a la escuela tienen más posibilidad de dar a luz a menos hijos, y poder criar a hijos más sanos y más educados. Los beneficios de esta educación pueden ir desde ser capaz de leer las instrucciones en las botellas de pastillas, de tomar mejores decisiones, hasta de poder conseguir un empleo.

La mayoría de los países están comprometidos a asegurar que todos los niños reciben alguna educación. Recientemente, Kenia de nuevo hizo gratuita la escuela primaria. No obstante, las niñas que desean asistir a la preparatoria, tienen que asistir a internados costosos. En la Isla de Vashon, las ventas de pasteles continúan; los estudiantes de la escuela secundaria también ayudan vendiendo pelotitas hacky sack.

Emma Bean compartió el sueño de sus condiscípulos: "Esperamos que, al ayudar a una parte del pueblo, podremos ayudar a la comunidad entera."

"Los niños son nuestro futuro," agregó Femke Oldham. "A ellos les damos la oportunidad de asegurar un futuro promisorio con muchas opciones."

Adaptación de un artículo de Lesley Reed

39

We have chosen and carefully edited articles that lend themselves to active reading, giving kids a great opportunity to annotate and work out their thinking as they read. Active literacy means you stop, think, and react to information as you read. We teach kids to code the text with their thinking: to underline important information, to star key ideas or points of interest, and to jot thoughts in the margins or on Post-its. When readers merge their thinking with the information, they learn, understand, and remember it.

We considered four primary factors in choosing these selections:

CONTENT. We looked for clear, engaging, well-presented information that kids can easily access and enjoy and we searched for articles with interesting themes and compelling topics to capture young, inquisitive minds.

FEATURES. We chose text that contains a variety of visual and text features including photographs, maps, charts, graphs, diagrams, titles, subheads, and more.

WRITING QUALITY. Frankly, we came across a lot of nonfiction for kids that is dull, mechanical, and voiceless. It doesn't have to be! For this collection, we searched for and found well-written selections that burst with vibrant language and active voice. Kids deserve good writing, too, so they can read and write engaging text.

READING LEVEL. For this resource, we chose texts of different lengths that cover a range of reading levels. *Toolkit Texts* includes three volumes designated for grades 2–3, 4–5, or 6–7. However, assigning a grade level to a particular text is arbitrary, particularly in nonfiction with all of its supportive features. So we suggest that you look carefully at all three volumes of *Toolkit Texts* and choose from them based on your kids' interests and tastes, as well as their reading levels. To differentiate text and reach the widest range of readers in your classroom, you may want to have two or three volumes at your fingertips.

These *Toolkit Texts* collections are full of text that kids can sink their teeth into including:

- a broad array of kid-friendly topics, from dinosaurs to hip-hop music, that appeal to the many diverse readers out there;

- topically related articles grouped together;

- a sampling of different nonfiction genres—feature articles, profiles, poems, letters, and more;

- a variety of science and social studies curricular topics, from space exploration to American history, common to American classrooms;

- a rich assortment of classic nonfiction text and visual features; and

- even some articles that build on topics introduced in *The Comprehension Toolkit*.

In addition, we have chosen some topics and themes that appear in all three volumes, making it easy for you to differentiate instruction with a variety of texts on similar themes. For example, there are articles about animals, ecology, sports, and Native Americans in all three volumes; paleontology, the ocean, and children with disabilities in Grades 2–3 and 4–5; and social and environmental change, education, American history, and ancient civilizations in both Grades 4–5 and 6–7.

How to Use These Articles

In *The Comprehension Toolkit*, we design instruction around the Gradual Release of Responsibility framework: teacher modeling, guided practice, collaborative practice, and independent practice. The articles in these volumes can be used to support any one of these phases of instruction. We can use them to model instruction by thinking aloud, reading aloud, and through shared reading. We can use them to model nonfiction writing strategies. If you are using *The Comprehension Toolkit*, feel free to substitute any of these articles for the *Toolkit* lesson texts, and then utilize the *Toolkit Lesson Guides* to facilitate *your* instruction. Suggestions for matching specific articles with comprehension strategies and *Toolkit* lessons follow on pages x through xii.

Kids get better at reading by reading, both with our support and on their own. We created this collection primarily because kids need terrific text to read independently both for enjoyment and for practice. But practice doesn't mean we just leave them to their own devices. We confer with individuals and meet with small groups for instruction and have selected these articles with both approaches in mind.

Strategies for Active Reading

Our approach to teaching comprehension focuses on a repertoire of cognitive strategies that proficient readers and thinkers use to construct meaning. We view these strategies as tools to be used flexibly and recursively according to the demands of the reading tasks, the text, and our purpose for reading it. In order to construct meaning and make sense of what we read, we have to monitor our comprehension by listening to the voice in our head. We might make connections, ask a few questions, or draw some inferences, all of which contribute to understanding information and ideas. An overview of reading comprehension strategies and how readers employ them follows.

MONITOR COMPREHENSION

- *listen to the inner voice and follow the inner conversation*

- *notice when meaning breaks down and/or mind wanders*

- *leave tracks of thinking by jotting thoughts when reading*

- *stop, think, and react to information*

- *talk about the reading before, during, and after reading*

- *respond to reading in writing*

- *employ "fix-up strategies"*—reread for clarification, read on to construct meaning, use context to break down an unfamiliar word, skip difficult parts, and continue on to see if meaning becomes clear, check and recheck answers and thinking, examine evidence

ACTIVATE AND CONNECT TO BACKGROUND KNOWLEDGE

- *refer to prior personal experience*

- *activate prior knowledge of the content, style, structure, features, genre, and so forth*

- *connect the new to the known*—use background knowledge to understand new information

- *merge thinking with new learning to build knowledge*

- *activate schema to read strategically*

ASK QUESTIONS

- *wonder about the content, concepts, outcomes, and genre*
- *question the author*
- *question the ideas and the information*
- *question to clarify confusion*
- *read to discover answers and gain information*
- *wonder about the text to understand big ideas*
- *do further research and investigation to gain information*

INFER AND VISUALIZE

- *use context clues to figure out the meaning of unfamiliar words*
- *draw conclusions from text evidence*
- *draw conclusions from text features*
- *predict outcomes, events, and characters' actions*
- *surface underlying themes*
- *answer questions that are not explicitly answered in the text*
- *create interpretations and sensory images based on the text, illustrations, and features*
- *visualize images and form impressions of the sensory content*

DETERMINE IMPORTANCE

- *sift important ideas from interesting but less important details*
- *target key information and code the text to hold thinking*
- *distinguish between what the reader thinks is important and what the author most wants the reader to take away*
- *construct main ideas from supporting details*
- *choose what to remember*

SUMMARIZE AND SYNTHESIZE

- *take stock of meaning while reading*
- *add to knowledge base*
- *paraphrase information*
- *move from facts to ideas*
- *use the parts to see the whole—read for the gist*
- *rethink misconceptions and tie opinions to the text*
- *revise thinking after reading*
- *merge what is known with new information to form a new idea, perspective or insight*
- *generate new knowledge*

Annotation as a Powerful Reading Tool

Recently we came across a document that Harvard University sends incoming freshmen to prepare them for academic life. "Interrogating Texts: Six Reading Habits to Develop in Your First Year at Harvard" describes reading behaviors that will help students get the most out of text. The suggestions include previewing, annotating, summarizing and analyzing, looking for patterns, contextualizing, and comparing and contrasting. All contribute to thoughtful reading. Here we share what Harvard has to say about *annotating*, because our *Toolkit Texts* offers a terrific opportunity for kids to merge their thinking with the information through annotation.

> *Make all of your reading thinking intensive. . . .*
>
> Mark up the margins of your text with WORDS: ideas that occur to you, notes about things that seem important to you, reminders of how issues in a text may connect with class discussion or course themes. This kind of interaction keeps you conscious of the REASON you are reading and the PURPOSES your instructor has in mind. Later in the term, when you are reviewing for a test or project, your marginalia will be useful memory triggers.
>
> Develop your own symbol system: asterisk a key idea, for example, or use an exclamation point for the surprising, absurd, bizarre. . . . Like your marginalia, your hieroglyphs can help you reconstruct the important observations that you made at an earlier time. And they will be indispensable when you return to a text later in the term, in search of a passage or an idea for a topic, or while preparing for an exam or project.
>
> Get in the habit of hearing yourself ask questions—"What does this mean?" "Why is he or she drawing that conclusion?" "Why is the class reading this text?" etc. Write the questions down (in your margins, at the beginning or end of the reading, in a notebook, or elsewhere). They are reminders of the unfinished business you still have with a text: something to ask during class discussion, or to come to terms with on your own, once you've had a chance to digest the material further, or have done further reading.
>
> http://hcl.harvard.edu/research/guides/lamont_handouts/interrogatingtexts.html

So we ask: why wait until our kids go off to college? We suggest kids read thoughtfully and leave tracks of their thinking as early as elementary school. Obviously elementary school kids cannot write in their books, but you can demonstrate how to use Post-its to annotate texts as they read, or provide photocopies of these articles on which they can write in the margins. The articles in this collection lend themselves to active reading and responding.

When we design instruction, we peel back the layers of our own reading process to decide what and how we need to teach with a particular text. So we have annotated an article here to show how we would model our thinking for our students.

First, we read through the entire piece ourselves, authentically responding to it by jotting our thinking in the margins or on Post-its when there is not enough room to annotate on the page. To think critically about important issues and ideas, we need to think and react in a thoughtful way as we read. We first consider our purpose for reading. It might be to answer a question, to pick out important information, or simply to learn more about a topic. We pay attention to our thinking, especially the strategies we use and the reactions we have, coding the text accordingly. Then when we teach, we think out loud as we read, demonstrating the strategies and language we use to understand.

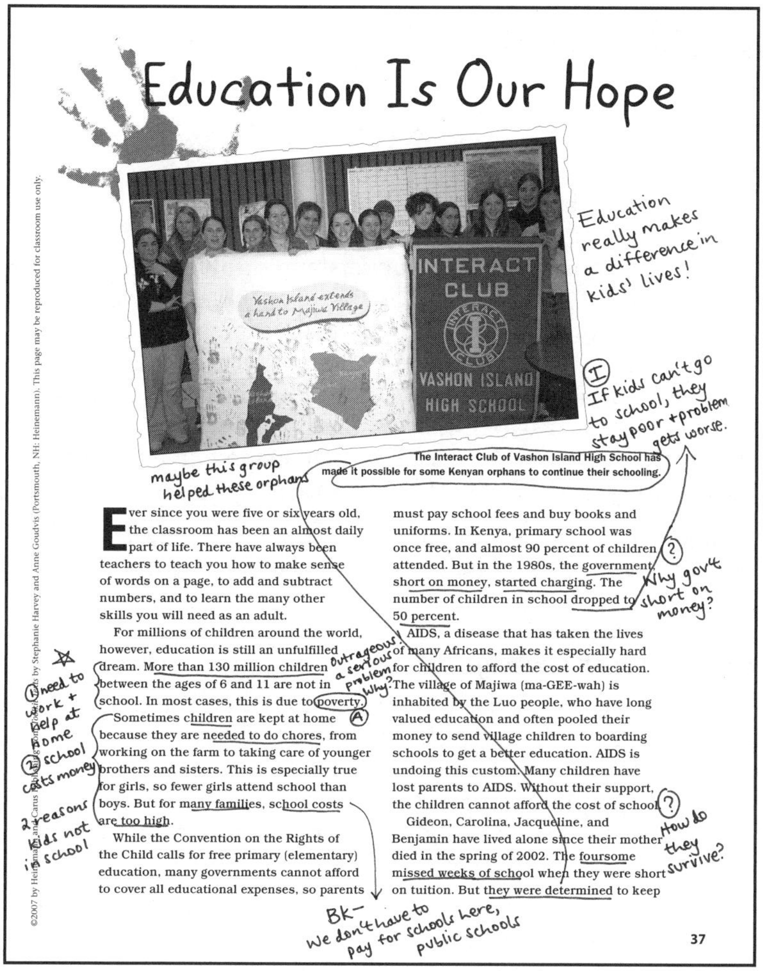

Education Is Our Hope

INTERACT CLUB
VASHON ISLAND HIGH SCHOOL
Education really makes a difference in kids' lives!
I If kids can't go to school, they stay poor + problem gets worse.
maybe this group helped these orphans
? Why gov't short on money?
Outrageous! a serious problem Why?
A
1 need to work + help at home
2 school costs money
2 reasons kids not in school
? How do they survive?
BK— We don't have to pay for schools here, public schools

The Interact Club of Vashon Island High School has made it possible for some Kenyan orphans to continue their schooling.

Ever since you were five or six years old, the classroom has been an almost daily part of life. There have always been teachers to teach you how to make sense of words on a page, to add and subtract numbers, and to learn the many other skills you will need as an adult.

For millions of children around the world, however, education is still an unfulfilled dream. More than 130 million children between the ages of 6 and 11 are not in school. In most cases, this is due to poverty.

Sometimes children are kept at home because they are needed to do chores, from working on the farm to taking care of younger brothers and sisters. This is especially true for girls, so fewer girls attend school than boys. But for many families, school costs are too high.

While the Convention on the Rights of the Child calls for free primary (elementary) education, many governments cannot afford to cover all educational expenses, so parents must pay school fees and buy books and uniforms. In Kenya, primary school was once free, and almost 90 percent of children attended. But in the 1980s, the government, short on money, started charging. The number of children in school dropped to 50 percent.

AIDS, a disease that has taken the lives of many Africans, makes it especially hard for children to afford the cost of education. The village of Majiwa (ma-GEE-wah) is inhabited by the Luo people, who have long valued education and often pooled their money to send village children to boarding schools to get a better education. AIDS is undoing this custom. Many children have lost parents to AIDS. Without their support, the children cannot afford the cost of school.

Gideon, Carolina, Jacqueline, and Benjamin have lived alone since their mother died in the spring of 2002. The foursome missed weeks of school when they were short on tuition. But they were determined to keep

37

As we read "Education Is Our Hope," we have reactions to the information that reflect our thoughts about the big idea here, which is that way too many kids around the world aren't in school. This is outrageous and our margin notes indicate that. As we read on, we have many questions that we might code with question marks. Some of our questions are answered in the article and some are not. We code those that are answered with an *A*, and we encourage kids to further investigate those questions that remain unanswered. We also draw conclusions and think inferentially to further our understanding, coding our inferences with an *I*. And we code very important information with a star or an asterisk. When reading information-packed text, we use a text codes and short jottings to record our thinking and make sense. We can't write too much or we would never get through the text. To get the most out of this article, we shared our reactions, asked questions, and made inferences.

Works Cited

Harvey, Stephanie, and Anne Goudvis. 2005. *The Comprehension Toolkit. Language and Lessons for Active Literacy.* Portsmouth, NH: Heinemann/Firsthand.

Harvey, Stephanie, and Anne Goudvis. 2007. *Strategies That Work: Teaching Comprehension for Understanding and Engagement.* Portland, ME: Stenhouse.

President and Fellows of Harvard College. 2007. *Interrogating Texts: Six Reading Habits to Develop in Your First Year at Harvard.* Available at: http://hcl.harvard.edu/research/guides/lamont_handouts/interrogatingtexts.html.

The Genre of Test Readings: Thoughtful Test Prep

In addition to providing guided and independent practice, the articles in these volumes may be used to help students prepare for high-stakes tests. The articles are quite similar to the selections that kids encounter on many state tests. To maximize the usefulness of these pieces when teaching the genre of test reading, first study the format and demands of your state test and develop practice lessons that parallel the structure of that exam. For a more detailed explanation of how to teach test reading as a genre, please see our test reading section on p. 74 in *Extend and Investigate* in *The Comprehension Toolkit*.

Building strong readers is still the best test preparation. Since prior knowledge is the most powerful determinant in reading comprehension, building background knowledge is ultimately the most direct route to raising scores. When kids read extensively across many topics and subject areas, they will add to their store of knowledge, which is one reason we urge our kids to read so much nonfiction.

Matching Comprehension Strategy Instruction to Text

On page xii, we have included a chart that correlates articles with specific strategies and *Toolkit* lessons. Every article requires readers to **Monitor Comprehension**. Monitoring comprehension is a thinking disposition. We monitor understanding and leave tracks of our thinking in everything we read. We simply can't make sense of any text if we don't keep track of our thinking as we go. Some texts, however, require readers to use a particular strategy above others to make meaning. So the chart reflects our suggestions for matching articles with specific strategies. And for those of you who are using *The Comprehension Toolkit*, the chart offers links to *Toolkit* lessons that dovetail nicely with certain articles. But above all, remember to trust your own judgment about the instruction your kids need and the articles that best serve those purposes.

If you decide you'd like to match more articles with a specific strategy to provide extra instruction or practice, that is easy to do. Here are some tips to help you narrow down your choices.

Activate and Connect to Background Knowledge

When you are trying to match the articles in this volume to the *activate and connect* strategy, we suggest you choose a topic about which kids are likely to have sufficient background knowledge. Familiar topics such as pets, sports, and music are included in this volume. After kids have been taught to connect the new to the known, they are more likely to activate their background knowledge to understand text that is less familiar.

Ask Questions

If you are looking for articles that fit well with the *questioning strategy*, you might choose text that is a little less familiar and nudges kids to wonder. Students ask questions to learn content and gain information. We also encourage kids to ask questions to clarify confusion and read to discover answers.

Infer and Visualize Meaning

When you want kids to *draw inferences*, consider choosing text that has some ambiguity, where all the information is not explicitly stated. The readers' task, then, is to combine their background knowledge with text clues to fill in the gaps and draw a conclusion about the information. Articles with prominent text and visual features support readers as they infer to understand information. When you want readers to *visualize* as they read, choose text where the writer shows rather than merely tells the ideas. When writers paint pictures with words, readers are more likely to visualize.

Determine Importance

It is hard to find a nonfiction text where *determining importance* is not a handy thing to do. But if you want your kids to practice this strategy explicitly, look for text that is packed with details so that readers have to sift out the most important information. Also, find text that is organized around sections with subheads, so kids can find the important information more readily.

Summarize and Synthesize

If you are searching for articles to teach your kids to *summarize and synthesize* information, many in this volume work. In truth, readers need to summarize and synthesize everything they read. However, when specifically teaching kids to summarize and synthesize, encourage them to tackle dense text with a lot of information. Articles that are packed with information require readers to get the gist, put the information into the own words, and sift out the bigger, more important ideas from a sea of facts.

All the articles in this collection were chosen for their versatility, and each one can be used to help kids learn or practice several comprehension strategies. But sometimes, certain strategies are more effective than others for digging out meaning. The corrrelation chart on the next page shows you which articles match best with particular strategies and points you to a specific lesson in our *Comprehension Toolkit* where you can see how we have taught that kind of thinking. Here's a list of the lessons from the *Toolkit*. (Harvey and Goudvis, 2004)

The Comprehension
Toolkit
Language and Lessons for Active Literacy

STRATEGY AND LESSON LIST

Cluster 1: Monitor Comprehension

1 Follow Your Inner Conversation
Listen to the voice in your head and leave tracks of your thinking

2 Notice When You Lose Your Way
Monitor your inner voice to focus your thinking

3 Read, Write, and Talk
Think your way through the text

Cluster 2: Activate and Connect

4 Follow the Text Signposts
Use nonfiction features to guide learning

5 Merge Your Thinking with New Learning
Read and think about new information

6 Connect the New to the Known
Activate and build background knowledge

Cluster 3: Ask Questions

7 Question the Text
Learn to ask questions as you read

8 Read to Discover Answers
Ask questions to gain information

9 Ask Questions to Expand Thinking
Wonder about the text to understand big ideas

Cluster 4: Infer and Visualize

10 Infer the Meaning of Unfamiliar Words
Use context clues to unpack vocabulary

11 Infer With Text Clues
Draw conclusions from text evidence

12 Tackle the Meaning of Language
Infer beyond the literal meaning

13 Crack Open Features
Infer the meaning of subheads and titles

14 Read With a Question in Mind
Infer to answer your questions

15 Wrap Your Mind Around the Big Ideas
Use text evidence to infer themes

Cluster 5: Determine Importance

16 Spotlight New Thinking
Learn to use a Fact/Question/Response chart

17 Record Important Ideas
Create an FQR with historical fiction

18 Target Key Information
Code the text to hold thinking

19 Determine What to Remember
Separate interesting details from important ideas

20 Distinguish Your Thinking From the Author's
Contrast what you think with the author's perspective

21 Construct Main Ideas From Supporting Details
Create a Topic/Detail/Response chart

Cluster 6: Summarize and Synthesize

22 Read, Think, and React
Paraphrase and respond to information

23 Think Beyond the Text
Move from facts to ideas

24 Read to Get the Gist
Synthesize your thinking as you go

25 Reread and Rethink
Rethink misconceptions and tie opinions to the text

26 Read, Write, and Reflect
Create a summary response to extend thinking

Correlation chart to strategies from
The Comprehension Toolkit

Read down the strategy column if you want to find *Toolkit Texts* articles for teaching or practicing a particular strategy. Read across the *Toolkit Texts* article row if you want to find particular strategies on which to focus instruction.

PAGE	Article Title	Monitor Comprehension	Activate & Connect	Ask Questions	Infer & Visualize	Determine Importance	Summarize & Synthesize
1	Bug Bites	●	●		TK LESSON 13		
4	How Do We Taste?	●			●		TK LESSON 24
7	Mystery Voices	●			●	TK LESSON 16	
8	Frog Watching	●			TK LESSON 14		
10	The Loch Ness Monster: Anatomy of a Hoax	●		TK LESSON 8		●	
12	On Deadly Ground: Storm Surge	●	●			TK LESSON 21	
14	Tornado!	●	TK LESSON 4				TK LESSON 22
17	Avalanche!	●			TK LESSON 13	TK LESSON 21	
18	Going Up: Life in the Death Zone	●		●		TK LESSON 18,19	
20	Basketball Without Borders: The Globalization of the NBA	●			TK LESSON 10		●
22	Watch Your Money Grow	●		TK LESSON 8			
24	Moneymakers	●	TK LESSON 4,5				
27	All Aboard the Underground Railroad	●			●	TK LESSON 18,19	
30	The Freedom to Learn	●	●			TK LESSON 16	
32	Stealing Freedom on the Underground Railroad	●			TK LESSON 13	●	
34	What is Child Labor?	●		●		TK LESSON 16	
37	Education Is Our Hope	●	●				TK LESSON 23
40	Hip-Hop at the Museum?	●	●				TK LESSON 24
42	Music to Your Ears . . . or Hearing Loss	●	TK LESSON 4				TK LESSON 22
44	Egypt: The Gift of the Nile	●	TK LESSON 6		●		
45	Help Wanted in Ancient Egypt	●			TK LESSON 13		●
46	All Wrapped Up: The Many Tasks of Mummy Makers	●		●			TK LESSON 24
50	Fun and Games in Early America	●	●			TK LESSON 18,19	
52	Getting Well: Healing the Sick in Early America	●	●			TK LESSON 18,19	
54	Navajo Code Talkers	●		●			TK LESSON 23,24
56	Viva La Causa: Chavez's Fight for Social Justice	●			TK LESSON 11	●	
60	"He Inspired Others": An Interview with Cesar's Grandson	●		TK LESSON 8			●
62	The Petticoat Vote	●		TK LESSON 9			
64	The Changing Face of American Voters	●					TK LESSON 22
66	A Long, Hard March	●			TK LESSON 15		

● The article works well with this strategy.

TK LESSON 7 The article works well with this *Toolkit* lesson.

Bug Bites

Two tarantulas, please. At a restaurant in Cambodia, Sok Khun samples deep-fried spiders. "This is a very normal food to eat," Khun says.

*Have you heard the one about the customer
who finds a fly in his soup?
Outraged, he points it out to the waiter, who says,
"Keep your voice down, or everybody'll want one!"
OK, so it's an old joke.
But the funny part is what the waiter says.
Who on earth would want to eat a bug?*

Well, would it surprise you if we said lots of people would? It's true. In Australia, South America, Africa, and Asia, eating bugs is no joke. Bugs aren't just pests. They're lunch or dinner or a nice after-school snack.

To those of us who've never crunched a cricket or slurped a worm, the idea of eating bugs sounds pretty gross. We wouldn't eat those creepy-crawlies even if someone dared us! Yet lots of bugs are nutritious, tasty, and perfectly safe to eat.

Eat Up! We're Outnumbered

Eating bugs is an old habit. Ten thousand years ago, before they learned to farm, our ancestors found food by hunting and gathering. Bugs were considered part of the daily diet. It made sense for ancient people to eat a source of nutrition that was right under their noses—or buzzing by their ears.

As you've probably noticed, bugs are everywhere. One out of every three animals is a bug, and scientists estimate that there are 200 million of the little critters for every person on the planet. No wonder more than half the people on earth still eat bugs daily. Of the million or so types of bug that scientists have named so far, more than 1,500 are somebody's favorite snack.

The most popular bugs to eat are crickets and termites, which are said to taste a bit like pineapple, but lots of other bugs are edible, too. Restaurants in Mexico sell ant tacos. Cans of baby bees line supermarket shelves in Japan. In Thailand, outdoor markets offer silkworm larvae. And in Mozambique, in eastern Africa, people call grasshoppers "flying shrimp."

Bugs Do a Body Good

Dinner is served: on one plate, a big, juicy hamburger, and on the other, a heaping pile of cooked grasshoppers. Ground beef or bugs? Which one do you think is better for your body?

Both have lots of protein, which is what your body uses to build muscle. But in other ways, grasshoppers clearly come out ahead. A pound of grasshoppers has less fat than a pound of beef, and the insects are higher in calcium and iron. Other bugs are good for you, too. Says biologist David George Gordon, author of the *Eat-a-Bug Cookbook,* "I tell kids, if your bones are still growing, eat more crickets and termites."

One scoop or two? Prossy Kasule sells dried grasshoppers at Nakasero Market in Uganda, a country in Africa. If grasshoppers don't make you jump for joy, stop in two stalls down for a bag of termites.

Not only are grasshoppers better for you than beef, they're also better for the planet. It takes a lot of grass and water and space to raise a cow. Imagine how many grasshoppers you could raise on the same amount of land!

Still wouldn't pick the grasshoppers? Gordon says they also taste delicious, a lot like green peppers.

A Matter of Taste

In North America and Europe, the idea of eating bugs is downright disgusting to most people. But even though we don't think of crickets and termites as food, lots of things we do eat are bug-related. Honey is made by bees. Shrimp, crayfish, crabs, and lobsters are all arthropods, which is what scientists call the bug group of animals. In fact, lobsters have only recently made the

Which Is More Nutritious—Ground Beef or Grasshoppers?

transition from bug to edible treat. The first American colonists ate lobsters only when they didn't have anything else. In Massachusetts, servants who were tired of getting the "cockroaches of the sea" for dinner wrote into their contracts that they'd eat lobster only three times a week.

Other parts of the world also have forbidden foods. Lots of people would never eat lobsters and the other sea-dwelling "bugs" we consider delicacies. Many people don't eat pork. Even among people who eat insects, tastes differ. South Africans might munch termites for lunch, but they'd never eat scorpions, which are raised for food in China. In Bali, Indonesia, dragonflies are a treat, but in the Indonesian province of Irian Jaya, no one would think of eating a dragonfly. Cicadas are on the menu instead.

So when it comes to eating, people mostly stick with food they're used to. What's food and what's not is a matter of taste—and what you've been taught.

Future Food

Could our tastes change? Could school lunches ever include grasshopper kabobs and caterpillar fritters?

Attitudes about bugs are already changing. Thanks to bug-appreciation programs at schools and science centers, kids today are less squeamish about insects. If we can get over the "Gross!" factor, bugs could one day become part of our daily diet. Bugs are even considered a perfect food for long space journeys, because astronauts could breed them in outer space.

Still wondering who on earth would want to eat a bug? Better to ask, who wouldn't?

Gotcha! On the island of Bali, kids catch dragonflies on long poles rubbed with sticky sap. This expert hunter (top) has skewered the day's catch on a strip of palm. Silly hats and ant casserole (right) are on the menu at the Roasted Goose restaurant in Kunming, China.

How Do We TASTE?

No, do not bite your little sister to find out. Instead, think about sweet hot fudge . . . salty, crunchy, munchy chips . . . sour, puckery lemons . . . a juicy, meaty hamburger . . . and (yech) bitter brewed tea. From these five basic tastes— sweet, salty, sour, savory, bitter—come all the flavors that we humans know and love (or hate). But how do we taste them?

I t all starts with your tongue. Check out your tongue in a mirror and notice its soft, velvety texture. Look more closely and you may see that it is actually covered with tiny points of flesh that give it a kind of shag-carpet look. Scattered around, mostly at the front, along the edges, and toward the back, you may see little bumps in various shapes. Inside these bumps are your taste buds, each one a collection of cells that are specially equipped to pick up the sweet, sour, bitter, savory, or salty flavors of the food you are chewing. (You also have taste buds on the roof of your mouth and inside your cheeks.) Humans are born with about 10,000 of these tiny taste-bud sense organs, and they work so hard that your body replaces them about every two weeks.

Other Taste Buddies

But taste buds don't do all the work. Suppose you are enjoying a spoonful of peanut butter. Remember that shag carpet on your tongue? Each of those tiny tabs of skin is actually designed to help your tongue feel the food in your mouth. They signal wildly to your brain about the thick, smooth, sticky substance that covers them. As you chew, the saliva in your mouth begins to digest the peanut butter with a special chemical. Soon, nothing

Thought your tongue was only good for sticking out? Read on. It helps you enjoy your favorite foods.

remains but microscopic particles of peanut butter. These come into contact with your taste buds, where special cells identify the taste of salt and the sweet taste of sugar (which are usually added to peanut butter). Nerves send this information on to your brain. At the same time, molecules carrying the fragrance of the peanut butter waft up through your nose, and scent detectors report the smell to your brain. Almost instantly, your brain gets all these messages and interprets them to recognize the flavor. WOW, it says, PEANUT BUTTER!

The combination of these characteristics—a food's basic tastes, the way it smells, and the feel of it in your mouth, along with its temperature and appearance— gives the food you eat its flavor. Believe it or not, smell accounts for about 85 percent of how something tastes.

If you try to eat your peanut butter sandwich while you are holding your nose (which isn't easy), you won't taste much.

Why Taste at All?

Why is the tasting process so complicated? Just so we can enjoy our food? There's more to it than that. In all animals, including humans, tasting does two important jobs: it warns us about bad foods and it attracts us to good ones. When our ancient ancestors roamed the forests and fields, hunting and gathering their dinner, they needed a way to tell poisonous plants from healthy ones, or whether a piece of meat was spoiled. In general, poisonous plants have a strong bitter flavor that both animals and people know to avoid. Because the taste buds on the back of the tongue are most sensitive to bitterness, even if you start to eat something bad, you have one last chance to gag and spit it out before you swallow. Similarly, spoiled food often tastes sour, warning us not to eat it. Sourness can also mean a food is not ripe and therefore not good to eat.

On the other hand, foods that contain certain amino acids, which are the building blocks of the proteins that our bodies require, have a savory, sort of meaty taste that humans like. Likewise, a pleasant, sweet taste is common in foods that are high in calories, which we need for energy. Early humans learned that sweet and savory tastes meant healthy foods. As a result, we still favor these tastes today. Indeed, human babies are born with a taste for sweetness to make sure that they will eat their first food, milk, which contains natural sugars.

Different Tastes for Different Folks

The world is full of wonderful things to eat. You probably have favorite foods and others you aren't so fond of. You and your best friend may disagree about what's better: chocolate mint ice cream or caramel vanilla. Why do our tastes differ so much? Tongues and taste buds are all the same, right? And the real stumper: Who does like the taste of broccoli anyway?

As scientists try to figure out how our sense of taste works, they are discovering that different people probably taste things differently because they have more or fewer taste buds. Most people, with an average number of buds, are medium tasters and enjoy a range of flavors and foods. (They, most likely, enjoy broccoli.) Certain people can't taste at all, which means that they probably don't enjoy eating anything and so may not be getting enough nutrition through their food. Their tongues have as few as 11 taste buds per square inch.

A frog's tongue actually faces the back of the mouth. It can flip forward and out in a split second to catch passing insects. The taste buds are located under the tongue.

Bees have taste buds in their legs and antennae to help them locate the nectar they love as they walk around a flower blossom.

Test Your Taste

About one in four people is a supertaster. Are you? Here's how to find out. You'll need a cotton swab, some blue food coloring, and a plastic reinforcement for three-hole binder paper. A magnifying glass might help, too.

1. Stand in front of the bathroom mirror and swipe a small drop of the food coloring on the front of your tongue with the cotton swab. Don't get the food coloring on anything else because it will stain.

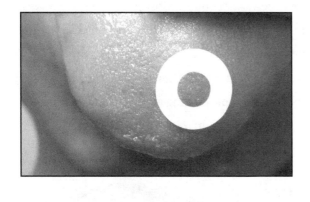

2. Rinse your mouth with clean water.

3. Place the reinforcement over the patch of food coloring on your tongue. Look closely in the mirror. (Use the magnifying glass if you need to.) The food coloring has turned most of the area blue, but the pink bumps you see (called papillae) contain taste buds.

4. Count the number of papillae inside the ring. If you have more than 25, you are probably a supertaster.

A third group of people are known as supertasters. These individuals can have 100 times more taste buds per square inch than nontasters do. This makes them extremely sensitive to certain tastes, and even temperatures, of food. Supertasters don't usually like spicy foods, and bitter or sour foods can have a very strong or unpleasant taste to them. Sweets may be just too rich tasting. Supertasters may not enjoy healthy foods such as grapefruit, broccoli, or celery because the taste is too strong.

Adapted from an article by Meg Moss

But don't worry; a little salt can make even supertasters enjoy their broccoli.

Chocolate? Yes, but without added sugar, it tastes bitter. It's good for cooking.

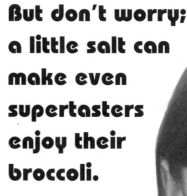

Catfish are equipped with taste buds all over their bodies to help them locate and identify food at the murky bottom of the lake. Their "whiskers," or barbels, alone have over 20,000 taste buds.

MYSTERY VOICES

Jeepers—It's a spring peeper!

They bark, peep, croak, quack, twang, trill, whistle, chirp, click, oink, snore, bleat, chuckle, grunt . . . and ribbit. And that's just the tip of the vocal iceberg for frogs.

Spring through summer, the rhythm of frog songs gives the night an audible pulse. Actually, what we hear are male frogs crooning for a mate, or telling other male frogs to keep away from their breeding ground. The range and variety of frog song is impressive, but what seems almost unbelievable is the volume.

Big Noises from Tiny Critters

Ever wonder how such tiny critters can make such loud noises? Many male frogs have a vocal sac—an expandable pouch full of elastic fibers—connected to the chin, beneath the floor of the mouth. (Some species have a sac on each side of the head.) The sac balloons out during vocalization. Does this mean, then, that the vocal sac is associated in some way with producing frog sound? No. A frog's vocal sac acts as a resonator for sound waves, meaning that the sac intensifies the sound that is first produced in the frog's vocal cords. The resonator (a frog's vocal sac) improves the ability of the frog to transmit sound in much the same way the wooden body of a guitar intensifies the sound created by its vibrating strings.

From Clicks to Trills

Frog calls range in duration from simple, brief clicks of 5 to 10 milliseconds to trills of several minutes. A long call is sustained by air being pushed back and forth across the larynx between the lungs and the vocal sac—in a manner similar to the way a bagpipe is played.

Here's how it works:

To vocalize, the frog first inflates its lungs, then expels the air through its larynx. The air rushes past the larynx and into the mouth, which the frog keeps closed. The air exits through tiny openings on the floor of the frog's mouth that lead into the vocal sac, causing it to expand. When the expansion reaches a certain level, the sac contracts due to the elastic properties of the tissue. The contraction pushes the air out through the larynx and into the lungs . . . which re-inflate. This cycle can continue with very little energy input because both structures, the sacs and the lungs, are highly elastic.

Spring peepers have one of the largest vocal-sac-to-body volume ratios of any of the frog species. The vocal sac is almost the same size as the peeper's body. It is part of a system that allows the frog to make repeated vocalizations without expending much energy. One peeper can repeat its call as often as 4,000 times per hour. Jeepers!

Adapted from an article by Stephen James O'Meara

Frog Watching

Long ago, people who worked deep in mines brought with them a canary in a cage. Canaries are very delicate—if the air in the mine became bad, the canary died. If that happened, the miners knew they needed to get out before the air got bad enough to harm them too. Frogs, and other creatures known as **amphibians,** are to the world like canaries are to a coal mine.

Sensitive Amphibians

Amphibians require both land and water environments to live. Their skin is very thin and porous. Their young hatch from eggs without shells. These characteristics make amphibians very sensitive to changes in their environment. Climate change or pollution affects them immediately. Therefore, they are among the first animals to die when the environment changes. In this way, frogs warn humans that something is wrong.

Something is wrong right now. Frogs and other amphibians are dying off at an alarming rate. They are also being born with deformities, such as extra legs. This tells us that there is a problem that is affecting their genes—those microscopic codes that tell the body how it is going to look. Normal frog genes do not include a code for five legs!

We do not have to wait for animals to become extinct to stop the problem. Over 200 species of amphibians around the world have experienced a fast drop in their populations. Imagine having 40 neighbors one summer and then the next summer you notice that you only have 12 neighbors left. That would be a fast decline in the population in your neighborhood. It would make you think something is wrong in your neighborhood, wouldn't it?

Why the Decline?

There are lots of explanations for why amphibians are dying off. We use a lot of pesticides on farm crops to kill bugs and prevent diseases. We use them in our backyards, too, to kill bugs in the flower and vegetable gardens or to kill weeds and grubs in our lawns. The overuse of pesticides has been proven to have a bad impact on animals.

Also, burning gasoline to run our cars and oil to heat our homes causes the earth's temperature to rise. This is known as **global warming.** Amphibians are affected by global warming.

The Golden Frog

The human population of the Latin American country Panama is growing rapidly. People need houses. Houses need land to sit on and lumber to make them. Both harvesting the lumber and clearing the land for houses and cattle ranches has changed the habitat of the Panamanian Golden Frog drastically and is thought to be in part responsible for the frog's decline in population.

Sadly, the Golden Frog's beautiful gold color adds to its decline—people like to collect them. Over-collection,

according to the website of Project Golden Frog, is a serious problem for the frog. The Golden Frog's dilemma is just one example of frog species in trouble all over the world.

Research

Scientists have been trying to figure out exactly what is affecting frogs and other amphibians in different parts of the world. They have gotten together in conferences to talk about it. Groups like FrogWatch and the National Amphibian Monitoring Project have started counting frogs each year. They keep an eye on amphibians around the world to see if the numbers get smaller from one year to the next.

What Can You Do to Help the Frogs?

What can be done? Some researchers are beginning to breed certain frog species in captivity to help save those that are threatened. We can all join in the effort of our own town's conservation commission to recognize important areas of land to conserve. We can then protect wildlife habitat and wetlands from becoming malls and housing developments by clustering houses and stores and leaving wide open spaces wherever possible. We can slow down the rate of global warming by creating and driving cars that use fuels other than gasoline—perhaps you can become the scientist that solves the world's global warming problem!

The Loch Ness Monster:

Nessie has made beautiful Loch Ness in Scotland famous. Proof of the monster's existence rests on shadowy images such as this one.

equally obscure evidence. None of it is convincing. So how can we explain 1,500 years of monster sightings? It's always best to investigate the original source of the legend.

Origin of a Myth

The Loch Ness Monster can be traced to A.D. 565, during the life of St. Columba, an Irish monk trying to convert the Scottish people into Christians. The story goes that St. Columba had witnessed the burial of a man killed by a "beast" in the Loch. Then he saw the monster rush another swimmer "with a great roaring and with a wide open mouth." St. Columba drove away the "beast" by making a sign of the cross and urging it to "think not to go further, touch not that man."

After translating and studying the original Latin text recounting St. Columba's experience, Charles Thomas, a professor at the University of Exeter, England, concluded that the "beast" was probably something like a walrus or a seal. Have you ever called your sister or brother a "beast" or a "monster" when they've done something bad? The "beast" in the Loch got its name the same way. End of story? It should have been, but . . .

The Footprint and the Photo

By 1933, stories about the Loch Ness Monster were accepted as myth—something fun to tell around a campfire. But in December 1933, Marmaduke Arundel Wetherell, a big-game hunter, discovered two footprints "less than a few hours old" on a beach at the Loch. Wetherell deduced that "a very powerful, soft-footed animal about 20 feet long" created them. Finally, evidence of a monster? Not at all. Plaster casts made of the footprints and studied by researchers of London's Natural History Museum revealed that the tracks were created by a hippo foot, not a mysterious creature. Someone created the footprints with a replica of a hippo foot, a common item used in

The cold waters of Loch Ness, Scotland's longest lake (38 kilometers or 24 miles), are home to one of the most enduring legends of our times—the Loch Ness Monster. Nessie, as the monster is commonly called, was first sighted as a "water beast" in the 6th century. Since then, it has been called a serpent, a dragon, a water-horse, and a prehistoric animal. But scientists call Nessie a myth of monstrous dimensions.

Let's cut to the chase. In the 1,500 years that Nessie's been around, there has been no solid evidence of its existence—nothing, say, like a corpse. We do have more than 3,000 eyewitness accounts, some poor-quality photographs, a movie clip showing an animated "blip," and some other

Anatomy of a Hoax

Divers deploy the "creature camera" to search for Nessie.

decorating in the early 1900s. The footprints were a hoax. Hopes for a monster sank like a stone dropped in the Loch.

The story would have ended there, but three months later the monster was captured "clearly" for the first time on film. The April 19, 1934, issue of London's *Daily Mail* published a photograph taken by Robert Kenneth Wilson, a respected London surgeon, which shows the monster's long neck and tiny head emerging out of the Loch's murky waters. That photo, known now as the "surgeon's photo," caused a wave of Nessie Fever. People no longer came to the Loch just to relax; they came to see the monster. The surgeon's photo was a boon for the tourist industry and the local economy. Nessie sightings, naturally, increased.

The Search

Scientists looking at the surgeon photo concluded it was indeed a photo . . . but of what? The grainy, shadowy form had nothing near it for scale. It could have been anything from gas bubbles to an elephant—and this remained the best photo. Then, in 1960, Nessie was filmed swimming. But when the Royal Air Force analyzed the film, they concluded only that something, probably a motorboat, was moving in the water.

Two ambitious scientific efforts to nab Nessie took place in the 1970s. Rob Rines, director of

the Academy of Applied Science in Boston, and Harold "Doc" Edgerton of MIT went to Scotland to photograph the monster underwater using automated cameras and side-scanning sonar—the same device used to discover the sunken *Titanic*. The sonar was so sensitive that it could detect objects hundreds of meters away on either side of the boat. The results? Merely shadows.

And the other expedition? In 1976, *National Geographic* placed highly sophisticated camera gear below the surface of the Loch and used recorded beeper sounds to attract the beast. They found, saw, and photographed . . . nothing.

The Confession

Nessie hysteria continued through 1994, with the surgeon's photo still the best evidence for a prehistoric animal in the Loch. But on March 12 of that year, The *London Sunday Telegraph* revealed the truth: The surgeon's "monster" was a small model made of plastic wood attached to a 35-cm toy submarine. The person who made the model, Christian Spurling, confessed that and more on his deathbed in 1993.

The "monster," he revealed, took eight days to make. The photo was not even taken by Dr. Wilson but by Spurling's stepbrother—Ian Wetherell, the son of the creator of the hippo-foot "monster footprints." Marmaduke Wetherell asked Spurling to make the model after the footprint fiasco; he was determined to give the public "their monster." Wilson was let in on the hoax because Wetherell knew Wilson's trusted name (not his) would give the photo credibility.

The hoax was done in "harmless fun." No one expected it would turn into a worldwide sensation. The situation got so out of control that all involved in the hoax decided to remain quiet about it. Wetherell and Wilson died with their mouths zipped shut. But Spurling had to clear his conscience. In doing so, he "killed" Nessie and 1,500 years of mystery.

Maybe it's best to end with a quote from the late astronomer, Carl Sagan: "There are wonders enough out there, without our inventing any."

Adapted from an article by Stephen James O'Meara

On Deadly Ground
STORM SURGE

In late August 2005, Hurricane Katrina slammed into Florida and the coastal regions of Alabama, Mississippi, and Louisiana. The most severe damage was to New Orleans— a city of some 500,000 people that lies six feet below sea level.

Storm-driven waters rushed inland and overflowed the system of **levees** that had, until then, protected the city from the Mississippi River and Lake Pontchartrain to the north. These levees, walls constructed to hold back water, were no match for the massive amount of water. The effects of the deluge were numbing. More than 650 people were dead and millions were homeless. Some 90,000 square miles—equivalent almost to the size of the United Kingdom (England, Wales, Scotland, and Northern Ireland)— were declared a federal disaster area. According to scientists at the National Oceanic and Atmospheric Administration's (NOAA's) National Climatic Data Center in Asheville, NC, Hurricane Katrina will be recorded as the most destructive storm ever in terms of economic loss, but not when measured in loss of life: The hurricane that hit Galveston, TX, in 1900 claimed between 6,000 and 12,000 victims. Still, the death toll now makes Katrina the 10th worst natural disaster to affect our nation.

Flood of Horror
Water (in this case a storm surge), more than wind, can turn a hurricane—an act of nature—into a human catastrophe.

"The greatest potential for loss of life related to a hurricane," says Brian Jarvinen, a forecaster and storm research specialist for the NOAA's National Hurricane Center, "is from the storm surge."

A storm surge is a hideous bulge of water—often 15 feet high and 50 miles wide—that forms directly beneath a hurricane's center, or eye (an area of extremely low air pressure). You can see how this works by holding a straw about 1/10 of an inch above a bowl of water, and then sucking hard. Water will be drawn up toward the base of the straw, which represents the eye of the hurricane.

The surge is propelled forward by the advancing storm and its intense winds. In the northern hemisphere, a hurricane rotates counterclockwise, so the greatest impacts from the storm surge tend to occur to the right of the eye at landfall. Intensified by the hammering effect of 15- to 20-foot breaking waves, the surge acts like a giant bulldozer and sweeps away everything in its path. Nine out of

ten deaths related to hurricanes are caused by the storm surge.

A Recipe for Disaster
When Katrina made landfall on August 29, the promise of a killer hurricane was delivered. At 7 A.M. a NOAA scientific buoy, located about 50 miles east of the mouth of the Mississippi River, recorded wave heights of at least 47 feet. Shortly thereafter, in a howling rage, Katrina smashed into the coast near New Orleans.

Using a Louisiana State University supercomputer, Joannes Westerink, an engineer at the University of Notre Dame, and his colleagues have recently created the first detailed computer model of the effects of Hurricane Katrina and its surge. In the 36 hours before Katrina hit New Orleans, the model shows a 15-foot dome of water forming in the Gulf of Mexico beneath the hurricane. The dome is being pushed forward by winds screaming at 140 miles per hour.

Levee—An embankment raised to prevent a river from overflowing

Dead fish in the floodwaters surround a worker as he repairs a levee in New Orleans.

On August 29, Destruction Day, the model shows the hurricane's northeasterly winds pushing a wall of water directly against the hurricane levees at the mouth of the Mississippi River, and then pouring over them. As the surge moves inland, it tops the hurricane levees that run toward the center of New Orleans. As Katrina moves toward Mississippi, the model shows a north wind pushing water in Lake Pontchartrain against south shore levees and into canals, where the rest of New Orleans floods as portions of the canal fail. Finally, the wave rises up 30 feet as it hits the Mississippi coast, where it causes massive destruction.

The Human Disaster

While the computer model has not solved any engineering problems, it is shedding some light on the cause of some of the resulting catastrophes. For instance, Westerink says that the surge may have raised the level of Lake Pontchartrain 12 feet or more, which could have been enough to top levees or floodwalls, which are built to withstand a maximum surge of only 11.5 feet.

The computer model is turning attention to the cause of the catastrophic collapse of several levees—ones that had been upgraded with a thick concrete wall!

The **irony** is that the Army Corps of Engineers strategically placed these levees and their concrete supports to prevent New Orleans from flooding. But according to the National Weather Service, over the almost three centuries (300 years) since the construction of the original levees along the river and lake, they have led to a *rise* in the water levels.

The result?

Each increase of water level puts more and more pressure on the levees. And while the levee system around New Orleans is quite extensive, it is old. The original structures, of which the Army Corps of engineers took possession, were built in *1718*! They had been built to withstand only what we now call a category 3 hurricane. Katrina was a category 4 hurricane.

The Power of Water

The power of water is extremely underestimated. Water weighs approximately 1,700 pounds per cubic

yard. It's so dense that it cannot be compressed. So when water hits an object (as when a storm surge pushes against a levee), the water does not absorb the shock of the impact by compressing. Instead, the object being struck usually yields to the force of the water. The levee breaks!

And that's a far more dangerous situation than if water were to simply overtop a levee. When a levee breaks, the water behind it is released as a flash flood, which is catastrophic to life and property because of the tremendous energy of the sudden release of an immense amount of water.

Maybe Katrina's real lesson is, Don't Fool with Mother Nature!

Irony—When what might be expected to happen and what actually occurs are inconsistent

---

The Saffir-Simpson Hurricane Scale

The Saffir-Simpson Hurricane Scale is a 1 to 5 rating based on a hurricane's intensity at the time of measurement. Wind speed is the determining factor in the scale.

Category One: Winds 74–95 mph. Storm surge generally 4 to 5 feet above normal.

Category Two: Winds 96–110 mph. Storm surge generally 6 to 8 feet above normal.

Category Three: Winds 111–130 mph. Storm surge generally 9 to 12 feet above normal.

Category Four: Winds 131–155 mph. Storm surge generally 13 to 18 feet above normal.

Category Five: Winds greater than 155 mph. Storm surge generally greater than 18 feet above normal.

Adapted from an article by Stephen James O'Meara

Tornado!

Weird Weather Week

In a state that averages 26 tornados annually, the tornado of May 4 was but one of 88 that swept through Missouri during a seven-day period in the spring of 2003. How could such a week happen?

Michael Hudson, meteorologist at the National Weather Service (NWS) office in Pleasant Hill, MO, says that the storm system on May 4 "was a textbook weather system. If you . . . were to draw up a weather map and put in all the elements that you need for severe weather—an extremely strong *jet stream,* lots of available heat and humidity from the Gulf of Mexico, cold air moving down from the northern plains and meeting up with this warm, juicy air over the area—all of these came together on May 4."

In fact, the NWS at Pleasant Hill was talking about the possibility of severe weather for several days prior to the tornado outbreak, and the Storm Prediction Center in Norman, OK, forecasted severe weather for much of the country. According to Hudson, on May 3 "they even listed specific cities. It was that clear-cut . . . that it was going to be a huge severe weather day."

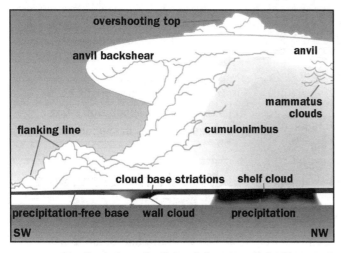

Idealized view of a "classic" supercell, looking west

Labels: overshooting top, anvil backshear, anvil, mammatus clouds, flanking line, cumulonimbus, cloud base striations, shelf cloud, precipitation-free base, wall cloud, precipitation, SW, NW

Anatomy of a Tornado

A *tornado* is a violently whirling column of wind that extends from the Earth's surface to the base of a thundercloud. How do you get a rotating column of air? This happens when a wall of warm, moist air meets a wall of cool, dry air. When these air masses collide, the warmer air goes up and the cool air goes under. Updrafts of warm air can reach wind speeds of over 100 mph, sending the warm, moist air miles up into the sky before colliding with the cooler jet stream.

This movement of air masses can create huge rotating storm clouds called *supercells,* resulting in severe weather—high winds, lightning, thunder, heavy

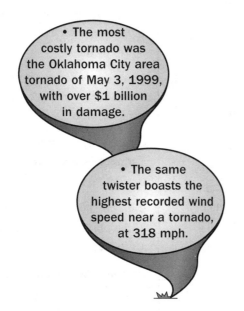

Jet stream—A meandering high-speed wind current, generally moving from a westerly direction at speeds often exceeding 250 miles per hour at altitudes of 10 to 15 miles

Twister Alert!

Tornado safety starts with knowing that a tornado is on its way, so stay informed and have a plan. If a twister is coming and you're in a building . . .

- **Find shelter!** If there is no basement, choose a closet, bathroom, or windowless room on the lowest floor, close to the center of the structure.

- **Take cover!** If you can, get under something sturdy. Make sure nothing heavy can fall on you. Crouch facedown, and cover the back of your neck and head with blankets, pillows, or your hands to protect yourself from flying objects—glass, metal, 2x4s, etc.

- **Keep them closed!** Opening doors and windows does not prevent damage, and exposes you to flying debris.

rains, and possibly hail (as moisture freezes in the upper atmosphere).

Meteorologists call the rotation in a supercell a *mesocyclone*. When this circular motion is picked up on radar screens, the NWS issues a tornado warning, which means that tornados could form and/or that one has been spotted on the ground.

Clouds swirling with rotating funnel clouds hanging down indicate that a tornado could form at any moment. Winds blowing in opposite directions around a strong updraft start a narrow, violent whirl. As centrifugal force throws the air away from the center, it leaves a core of very low pressure, which acts as a powerful vacuum.

The first sign of a tornado may be a strong whirlwind of dust from the ground's surface. Often, at the same time, a short funnel grows from the storm cloud above it. The funnel becomes more organized, connecting with the rotating column on the ground—and a tornado is born.

> • The usual tracking speed of a twister is 35 mph, but some have reached 65 mph.

Tracking the Beast

With Doppler radar linked to a bank of computers, the NWS has the capability of detecting supercell thunderstorms and tracking their movement. Doppler radar runs in two modes. In one, the storm reflects energy back to the radar showing how intense the storm is. The second is much like police radar—a beam is sent out and bounces back with a different frequency. The change in frequency allows the radar to determine movement toward or away from the radar, thus detecting rotation in the supercell.

The NWS also utilizes data from weather satellites. But even with all these up-to-date methods and equipment, human beings are still a vital part of severe weather prediction and early warning. People are needed to interpret the information, and storm spotters and chasers are needed at the scene.

Spotters and chasers? These aren't just thrill-seekers out to see how close they can get to a tornado without being swallowed up. These people have been trained to assess the elements of supercells and identify tornadoes as they form. Spotters follow storms to watch for this development. They have also been taught how to "chase" a storm, while leaving themselves an escape route should the monster winds turn toward them.

This exciting and dangerous aspect of weather watching plays an integral part in the safety of many communities. The spotters and chasers relay their information to the National Weather Service, which turns it into reports and broadcasts these updates on the emergency broadcasting network and National Oceanographic and Atmospheric Administration (NOAA) weather radio stations.

> • The average number of tornados per year in the United States: 1,000.

Tornadoes' Weird Ways

Here are some strange-but-true tales from the Missouri tornadoes:

- A china hutch was left untouched in a house that was otherwise leveled to its foundation.
- Items were carried over 100 miles away and then deposited unharmed.
- A semitrailer truck was emptied of its load, lifted over 300 feet into the air, and set down without damage.
- Cattle were moved to neighboring fields.
- A grand piano was carried a quarter of a mile.
- Mature trees were uprooted and planted in the middle of paved roads.
- Straws were driven into trees, and boards were pounded several feet into the ground.

• The tallest tornado, at 10,800 feet, occurred in the Unita Mountains of Utah.

The Shape of Things to Come

The spring of 2003's deadly tornado spree makes you wonder, What will this year be like? Let's hope it won't be as bad as May 2003.

Mike Hudson says, "2003 certainly was a very extreme year. But you can look back to the 1950s. You can look back to 1965, 1974—there are other years in our climatology that also were extreme severe weather years. On May 4, 1977, there was actually a bigger tornado outbreak right here around the Kansas City area than May 4, 2003, had," he says.

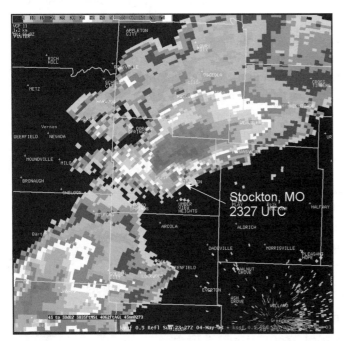

Stockton, MO
2327 UTC

NWS Doppler radar view

According to Hudson, in order to identify a trend toward more active or severe weather, you must look at long periods of time—30 to 40 years.

Accurate long-range forecasts are difficult because weather itself is *volatile*—subject to change at any time. By taking a collection of data on present weather, using mathematical equations and physics, observing global weather conditions such as ocean temperatures, and including the personal experience of forecasters, meteorologists make the best projections they can. However, even the most careful predictions may not end up being accurate.

Looking Ahead

Back in the town of Stockton, MO, the sun is shining. The heat of summer softens the memory of the monster tornado that swept through this sleepy town not that long ago. Residents are still cleaning up debris and rebuilding their homes. When the coming spring begins to brew up another season of supercell thunder storms, you can be sure that they will be keeping a "weather eye" open for another twister. But meanwhile, life goes on and life is good.

• Big, fat tornadoes aren't always the strongest.

Adapted from an article by Leslie J. Wyatt

AVALANCHE!

When snow on a slope gives in to gravity, we know it as an avalanche. Avalanches happen naturally or they are triggered by people—skiers, snowboarders, hikers, snowmobilers, or anyone who is out in mountainous areas in the winter.

Types of Avalanches

There are a few different types of avalanches. The "loose snow" avalanche is fresh snow that spreads out as it tumbles down the mountain, so it rarely gets deep enough to bury someone. "Ice fall" avalanches occur on glaciers, when a chunk of glacier separates from another and drops steeply. There is even the "roof avalanche," when snow built up on the roof of a house slides off. It can be dangerous if you happen to walk by just as the mass of snow begins to fall!

The Most Dangerous Avalanche

The type of avalanche of greatest concern to hikers and skiers is the "slab avalanche," which is when a huge chunk of snow comes plummeting down a mountainside in one piece. One of the reasons it is so dangerous is that there are few visible telltale signs that an area may have an avalanche.

A slab avalanche can reach speeds as high as 120 miles per hour. The speed and force of the snow hurtling down the mountain that fast can hurt a person in its path. But often people are most in danger from the debris that comes down along with the snow—trees, rocks, and even your own ski equipment turn into lethal weapons. If you survive all that, suffocation becomes your next problem. The snow can bury you completely. And during the avalanche, the snow compresses so much that you can't move if you are buried.

Avalanche Recipe

Scientists who study avalanches have determined there are three ingredients necessary to create an avalanche: snowpack, terrain, and weather. These three factors are known as the "avalanche triangle."

The bond between the different layers of snow, or the "snowpack," influences if and when a slope of snow will go sliding down the hill. The weather conditions as the snowpack has built up will also impact how the snow on the slope holds together. And finally, the angle of a slope, the direction the slope faces, and the amount of sun that shines on it during the day all determine the likelihood and the severity of an avalanche.

The Noise Myth

Loud noises do not trigger avalanches. What does trigger them is a sudden increase in weight in just the right area. Ninety percent of avalanches are triggered by the person who gets buried, or by someone who is with that person. Just the weight of one person stepping on just the right spot on a slope of snow can cause the slab of snow to start sliding!

Sadly, the statistics for getting safely dug out of an avalanche are not good. If people with you can dig you out in 15 minutes or less, your chance of survival is excellent. After a half an hour, your chance of survival is very poor.

What Can You Do?

First, never hike or ski alone. Carry rescue equipment with you. And learn to read the signs of a potential avalanche so the weight of your own body doesn't turn it into a real avalanche!

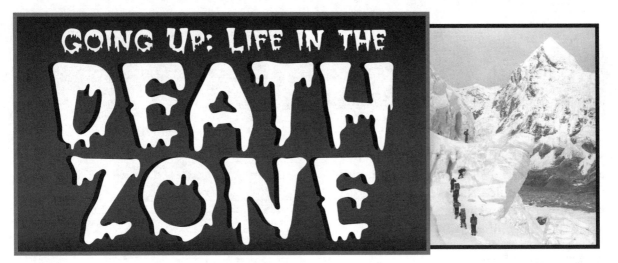

GOING UP: LIFE IN THE DEATH ZONE

The New Zealander struggled up the final snowy ridge. His companion soon joined him on the mountaintop, gasping for breath. Edmund Hillary offered his hand to Tenzing Norgay, but Norgay gave him a bear hug instead.

Fifty years ago, Hillary and Norgay became the first to reach the summit of Mt. Everest. Since 1953, the mountain has been climbed many times. The death toll is 175 for those who didn't make it to the top. Many were killed not by falls or avalanches, but by the effects of low pressure at extreme altitudes.

Going Up into Thinner Air

The weight of the atmosphere creates air pressure. At higher altitudes, there is less air above you. This means that the density and pressure of air *decreases* as altitude *increases*. Each intake of air on Mt. Everest has only one-third of the gas molecules—including oxygen—that would be present at sea level.

Mt. Everest is in Nepal, a small country sandwiched between India and China. Nepal's capital, Kathmandu, is at 1,340 meters (4,400 feet) —not much higher than Salt Lake City, UT. Unless exercising hard, a person in Kathmandu probably wouldn't notice the slightly thinner air.

Less Oxygen Equals More Work

However, as you move higher, the body reacts to the decreasing pressure. On their way to Everest, Hillary and Norgay stayed at Namche Bazaar, a trading town at 3,440 meters (11,300 feet). With each breath at Namche Bazaar, the body takes in only 70 percent of the oxygen it would get at sea level.

In response, the body makes more red blood cells that carry oxygen throughout the body. More red blood cells mean that more oxygen can be pulled from the thin atmosphere. Breathing automatically speeds up, and the heart beats faster as the body tries to get the oxygen it needs.

It takes many days for the body to make the extra red blood cells. Allowing the body to adjust slowly to the lower air pressure at high altitudes is called *acclimatization*. Hillary and Norgay spent many weeks acclimatizing to higher altitudes. Rushing up and down Mt. Everest isn't an option. A person taken directly from sea level to the summit would die of oxygen starvation within minutes due to a lack of enough red blood cells to pull oxygen from the thin atmosphere.

Reaching Base Camp

From Namche Bazaar, Hillary, Norgay, and their team trekked to the Mt. Everest base camp at 5,364 meters (17,600 feet), where most of their supplies were kept. At this altitude, air pressure is half that of sea level. Even with acclimatization, some people show signs of mountain sickness, caused by too little oxygen, which can result in headaches, dizziness, and fatigue.

Fluid buildup in the lungs and brain is also a threat. For reasons not well understood, lower air pressure causes fluid to leak from tiny blood vessels, called *capillaries*, in

An oxygen supply is crucial to climbing Everest. Early equipment was cumbersome.

Modern-day ascenders of Mt. Everest have sophisticated clothing and equipment to help them make it in and out of the Death Zone.

Above 8,000 meters, the human body "hits the wall." Bottled oxygen can hold off acute mountain sickness, pulmonary edema, and cerebral edema, but only temporarily. If a climber stays above 8,000 meters too long, death is inevitable. It's a brutal race against time. Can the climber get to the top and back before the body falls apart?

When Hillary was in the Death Zone, it took "three hours to do what I could have done in half an hour at sea level . . . every step became . . . [a] major task that was going to require a maximum of effort." On the last climb to the summit, "I seemed clumsy and unstable, and my breath was hurried and uneven."

the body. Fluid in the lungs, known as *pulmonary edema*, keeps desperately needed oxygen from getting to the muscles and brain, causing weakness and confusion. Fluid leaking into the brain, *cerebral edema*, causes dangerous swelling, hallucinations, and irrational behavior. Both pulmonary and cerebral edema can kill. The only cure is retreating to a lower altitude.

A Triumphant Ascent

Hillary and Norgay reached the top and took off their oxygen masks for a few moments. They were too tired to do more than hug and take photographs. When Hillary tried to put the camera away, he realized that a lack of oxygen to his brain was causing his slow, fumbling movements. Hillary and Norgay strapped on their oxygen masks and started their journey down.

Bottled Oxygen: A Climber's Life Line

Hillary and Norgay helped move loads of supplies from the base camp to camps higher on the mountain, breathing bottled oxygen to help offset the thin air. "As the oxygen flowed into my lungs, my load seemed to lose half its weight," wrote Hillary. After 44 days of acclimatizing on Everest's slopes, Hillary and Norgay climbed above 8,000 meters (26,250 feet) into the Death Zone.

As Hillary and Norgay descended the mountain, they were joined along the way by expedition members who had stayed at lower camps. As they neared one camp, they could see the question on the members' faces: Had they reached the top?

A companion walking down with Hillary and Norgay joyfully pointed toward the summit. Their faces "lighting up with unbelieving joy," the men in camp rushed toward Hillary and Norgay.

It was a long, tiring, triumphant walk home.

Adapted from an article by Pamela S. Turner

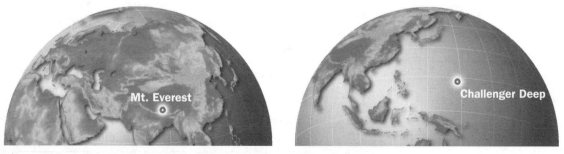

The Greatest Ups and Downs

- **Highest spot on Earth: Mt. Everest**
  Elevation: 8,850 meters (29,035 feet) above sea level
  Pressure at the summit: $\frac{1}{3}$ of an atmosphere
  Number of people who've been there: 1,200 (and climbing)

- **Lowest spot on Earth: Challenger Deep** (off the Mariana Islands)
  Elevation: 10,091 meters (33,100 feet) below sea level
  Pressure at the bottom: 1,010 atmospheres
  Number of people who've been there: 2

P.S.T.

That familiar orange ball can be seen in play even in Tibet.

China's Yao Ming is more than just a basketball player who stands seven feet five inches tall. He is also an example of **globalization** in America's National Basketball Association (NBA).

The Houston Rockets chose Ming as their number one draft choice in 2002. Being drafted by the Rockets didn't mean that Ming could hop the first plane from China to Houston. He could leave China only if he had his government's permission. That left the Chinese government with quite a dilemma. They had to decide whether to let Ming go to the United States.

It was a classic globalization story in which a country had to decide whether it was in their best interest to let go of a valuable resource. In this case, the resource was Ming.

After much negotiating, the Chinese government allowed Ming to go to Houston. They brokered a deal that would benefit their country financially and, more importantly, grow their country's basketball program. The Rockets agreed to train members of Ming's Chinese team, the Shanghai Sharks, alongside their own players during the off-season. The deal gave Chinese athletes access to some of the best coaches in the world of basketball.

The Chinese government also required Ming to give them half of his salary. On top of that, he also had to agree to pay Chinese taxes on his salary and give a percentage of his earnings to the Shanghai Sharks.

China benefited more than just monetarily from their decision to release Ming to the United States. As China's one billion citizens watched Ming excel in the NBA, they became more interested in their own country's basketball teams. That was important to the Chinese government because

> **Globalization: The process of spreading objects and experiences to all people at all corners of the earth.**

Basketball Without Borders
The Globalization of the NBA

The NBA recruits basketball players all over the world—including Yao Ming, from China. Here, Ming receives a gift from Sheikh Saud Bin Ali Al-Thani after a game in Japan.

they strive to build **nationalism** through sports. They believe that this will lead to more pride and **patriotism** among their citizens.

Ming is not the only foreign-born player in the NBA. There were 82 international players from 38 countries on the official rosters for the NBA's 2005-2006 season. Compare this to the six international players on the rosters in 1979.

The number of international players in the league began to grow in 1989 after professional basketball players were no longer barred from competing in the Olympics. This opened the door for international players to play for both the NBA and their country's Olympic basketball team.

After this, NBA teams began drafting globally and allocating large amounts of money to their international scouting budgets. The NBA also established offices in Europe, Australia, and Asia. They realized that by tapping a global market they could choose players from a larger pool of talent.

Expanding into a global market has made the NBA popular throughout the world. Games are seen in 750 million households in 212 countries. This has led to a worldwide extension of American culture that has benefited many U.S. companies, including sneaker manufacturers.

Not everyone is as happy as those sneaker companies. Some critics of the NBA's globalization feel that the sport is being stripped of its "Americanism." They believe that basketball becomes less engaging here at home as more international players take the place of Americans. Some American players take jobs with European teams. More than one critic has suggested following China's lead and limiting the number of foreign-born players on each NBA team. China allows no more than two international players on each of its basketball teams.

Supporters of globalization argue that the popularity of basketball increased dramatically after the heavy recruitment of international players began. They believe that these players have only improved the game and made it more exciting.

There is no doubt that the debate over the globalization of the NBA will continue. In the meantime, the many talented international players will continue to do what they do best: shoot, block, rebound, and score.

Adapted from an article by Christine Graf

> **Nationalism:** Loyalty to one's own country
> **Patriotism:** Great love for one's country

WATCH YOUR MONEY GROW

Have you ever heard ads by banks saying that they can help your money "grow"? Did you think that was strange? After all, money doesn't grow in the same way that plants do, with water and sunshine. Money grows when you save some regularly.

There are many reasons to save money. (When you "save" money, you wait until later to spend it.) Grown-ups save their money to buy expensive things like cars, or so they can take a trip, or for

2% of $100 = $2

What is interest?

A bank pays you interest in order to be able to use your money. People who borrow money from the bank pay interest for the privilege of using someone else's money.

Confused?

Here's how it works:

$ Lorenzo opens a savings account by putting $100 in the bank.

$ The bank pays Lorenzo 2 percent interest for the privilege of using his money. (Two percent of $100 is $2.)

emergencies. Kids also save money to buy things. Sometimes they save for college.

There are many ways to save money. Some people put their money into a piggy bank or hide it under a mattress. A smarter place to save your money is in a bank.

When you let a bank keep your money safe, a funny thing happens. The bank lends your money to other people. Don't worry; you still can get your money whenever you need it. But the bank pays you for using your money. The money they pay you is called interest. The bank earns interest, too, when it lends your money out.

So if you want to sit back and watch your money grow, start by putting what you have into the bank. Then, do some chores or other work and add your hard-earned dollars to your bank account.

Adapted from an article by Barbara Hagen
Illustrated by Patty Weise

$ Janeen comes to the bank to take out a loan for $100. The bank lends Lorenzo's money to Janeen and charges her 10 percent interest.

$ Janeen pays the bank back the $100 she borrowed, plus the 10 percent interest, for a total of $110.

(In other words, it cost Janeen $10 to borrow that $100 from the bank.)

$ Janeen paid $10 for the privilege of borrowing money, Lorenzo earned $2 for allowing the bank to use his money, and the bank earned $8 for managing the transactions.

 Moneymakers

Some people make their money by making money. If that sounds strange, think of it this way: The people who work for the Bureau of Engraving and Printing (BEP) of the U.S. Department of the Treasury actually make money. Their job is to print all the paper dollars we use in the United States. When the BEP began in 1862, it was a single room in the basement of the Treasury building. Today, 2,600 people in Washington, D.C., and Fort Worth, Texas, work for the BEP, printing more than 6,000,000 bills each month!

Making money is a complicated process: Bills are designed. Metal plates for printing are made. Bills are printed on sheets and then cut. In fact, there are more than 65 steps in the process of making paper money. Along the way, the money is examined many times for problems or mistakes. (With 65 steps, there is a lot of room for error.)

MONEY MATH

Using a super-fast printing press, the BEP can print about 8,000 sheets of bills per hour. With 32 bills to a sheet, that's 256,000 bills per hour. For $1 bills, that means $256,000 per hour. Try multiplying 256,000 bills by $5, $20, and $100. Then do a little more math to see how much money can be made in an 8-hour day. Whew! That's a lot of cash. (For $1 bills, that's 256,000 bills per hour x $1 per bill x 8 hours = $2,048,000 in one 8-hour day.)

Inspecting sheets of newly printed $1 bills

MINTING MONEY

What about coins? All of the coins issued by the U.S. government are made by the United States Mint. The two largest mints—in Denver and Philadelphia—make 65 to 80 million coins every day! Beginning in 1999, the Mint has issued five new quarters each year to honor five different states. By 2008, there will be 50 state quarters.

If you want to start collecting coins, the state quarters are a good place to start. Then you'll be a numismatist (say new-MISS-ma-tist), a coin collector.

Newly minted pennies

No Fake Bills

What do special paper (made of linen and cotton), color-shifting inks, security threads, and micro-printing have in common? They are all methods used by the BEP to stop people from making fake bills. Counterfeiting, or illegally making fake money, is a crime. Anyone caught doing it can go to jail.

With today's easy access to color photocopiers, the BEP had to come up with security features that don't copy well. Take a close look at a $5.00 bill. Hold it up to the light. Can you see an image of Abraham Lincoln in the lower right-hand corner? This is a security feature. Tiny red and blue threads run through the bills; some of the inks change color as you look at them from different angles; and what appear to be thin lines are actually tiny words that can be read only with a magnifying glass. None of these things show up in counterfeit, photocopied bills.

FUN FACTS

The largest denomination of bills printed today is $100. Bills for $500, $1,000, $5,000, and $10,000 exist too, but no new ones have been printed for many years.

As strong as paper money is, most $1 bills last only 18 months. Bills for $5 and $10 last about the same time; larger denominations last longer.

Find out more by taking a tour of the BEP at www.moneyfactory.com and explore the U.S. Mint at www.usmint.gov//kids

When money gets too old or is torn, burned, or otherwise damaged, you can turn it in to the BEP for a crisp, new bill. If there is less than half of the bill left, you must show proof that the other half was destroyed.

Every year, people cash in more than $30,000,000 in damaged currency for new bills. The Department of the Treasury shreds the old bills. So if you ever find a buried box of money, even if it's waterlogged or chewed by mice, you know what to do with it.

Adapted from an article by Amanda Yskamp

Introducing the new $20 bill with improved security features

All Aboard
the Underground Railroad

Escaping slaves often had to work their way through slaveholding states and live off the land before they reached safe stops on the Underground Railroad. These runaway slaves in Virginia's Great Dismal Swamp are being chased by dogs.

Many myths surround the Underground Railroad. The two biggest misconceptions are that it actually was a system of tracks along which trains rode and that it ran below the earth. The Underground Railroad was neither.

Thousands Working for Freedom

In reality, the Underground Railroad was a loosely organized group of people working simply but courageously *against* slavery and *for* the freedom of those bound to servitude. Involved in the Underground Railroad system were those running away from their enslavement and those helping the individuals who chose to escape. It is believed that as many as 100,000 slaves escaped on the Railroad. They were helped by at least three to four thousand "conductors." The system operated from the early 1800s through the start of the Civil War.

African Americans caught in the system of slavery were the key participants in this movement—most were young and male. They ranged from field workers to house slaves to skilled craftspeople. But all shared the desire to be free.

A Great Risk for Freedom

Escaping from slavery meant taking a tremendous risk. If successful, the runaways might never see their families or loved ones again. Leaving behind children or parents or siblings made the decision to escape a painful one.

And if an escape attempt failed and resulted in capture, *fugitive* slaves faced severe punishment. Slave owners sought to make examples of escapees as a way of discouraging others from trying to get free. Descriptions of the whippings given captured slaves or the devices put on them to prevent another escape are graphic and frightening.

In an attempt to make escaping to freedom in the North even more difficult, some runaways were sold to new masters who lived farther south.

Fugitive means running away or fleeing from the law.

Biased means marked by prejudice.

Quakers are members of the religious group also known as the Society of Friends, who reject violence.

Refuge is a place that provides protection from danger.

The people who chose to aid runaway slaves also faced great risks. Fugitive slave laws existed that supported the rights of slaveholders. Anyone found helping escaped slaves was given a heavy fine, had property taken away, and could be sent to jail. In fact, the system that put both runaways and helpers on trial was *biased* in that it paid judges more if the accused were found guilty.

Actively Working for Justice

Yet, even with those discouragements, many people were active in the Underground Railroad, including free African Americans, abolitionists, other slaves, *Quakers* and other religious groups, and American Indians. All were opposed to the enslavement of human beings.

Their support came in many forms. Conductors on the Underground Railroad assisted with food, *refuge,* and instructions to the next safe stopping place. Homes, barns, and other buildings—referred to as stations or stops—often had hidden areas beneath floors or behind walls that allowed

Attempting an escape involved great risks, but some slaves were willing to face them rather than remain in bondage.

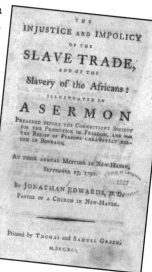

As early as 1791, theologian Jonathan Edwards preached against the slave trade.

runaways to rest and eat before they continued on their journey. When angry slave owners or slave catchers were in close pursuit, these secure havens hid the fugitives and made capture more difficult.

Secrecy Meant Safety and Success

Contrary to popular belief, the Underground Railroad system was not run or operated by a strictly established organization. Nor was it a nationwide operation. Usually, individuals in a particular region knew of others to whom they could send the escaping slaves. Given the dangers of participating in the Under-ground Railroad, many people chose to keep their involvement secret or known to only a few others. This kept them safer, while making it harder for outsiders to understand how the system worked in their area. Secrecy played an integral part in the success of the Underground Railroad.

Sharing the story of the Underground Railroad is significant because its participants offer a powerful example. Their courage, cooperation, and perseverance illustrate the impact individuals can have when they take a stand for what they believe is right. Members of the Underground Railroad highlight the importance of freedom as a basic American principle and the necessity of protecting it for all citizens. Their efforts made a difference in history and remind us of the differences we, too, can make today.

Adapted from an article by Spencer R. Crew

DEFINING SPECIAL TERMS

Here are some key words used by those involved in the Underground Railroad system. As you read them, notice how the participants used train-related terminology in their own unique way. Railroad trains were new methods of transportation in the 1830s and 1840s. The terms associated with this new invention became useful code words on the Underground Railroad.

Conductors provided food, shelter, and directions to runaway slaves and led them from one station to another.

Heaven, the **Promised Land,** or **Canaan** referred to Canada.

Passengers, cargoes, or **packages** meant fugitive slaves.

Routes or **rails** were the many different paths—some by land, some by water—that escaping slaves took to reach freedom.

Stations or **stops** were safe houses, or hiding places, for the runaways. These included buildings such as churches, homes, and barns.

The **stationmaster** was the person in charge of the hiding place.

The Freedom TO LEARN

Contraband means smuggled goods. During the Civil War, it was a term used to describe an escaped slave behind Union lines.

Whenever Union soldiers from the North marched into one of the Confederate states in the South and claimed territory, slaves ran to them for protection from Southern slave owners. Considered *contraband,* they often lived in little towns called "contraband camps." These camps usually were found near where the Union army had set up its tents.

The former slaves lived in old packing crates, sod huts, and—if they were lucky— abandoned houses. One room might hold as many as six families. Children, like their parents, worked very hard. They planted and harvested crops, worked as servants to soldiers, or took care of younger brothers and sisters. It was a rough introduction to freedom.

But most black children did manage to spend at least part of their time in school. Some worked in the morning and attended class in the afternoon. Young babysitters brought their infant and toddler siblings with them to school, letting them nap on the porch while the older brothers and sisters studied inside.

Some schools were very small, like the one organized for several little black girls by the nine-year-old daughter of a Union army surgeon in Corinth, Mississippi. Others were quite large. For instance, fourteen hundred African American students attended public schools run by the Union army in New Orleans. And a woman named Lucy Chase opened a school in Richmond's (Virginia) First African Church that had more than one thousand students!

Some teachers were African Americans, and some were former slaves. In 1861, Mary Smith Peake organized the first school opened by the American Missionary Association in Norfolk, Virginia. Peake was a black woman whose school eventually became the

Hampton Institute (now Hampton University). Many nineteenth-century and early twentieth-century black leaders, such as Booker T. Washington, were educated there.

The subjects learned by these newly freed children were often the same as those studied by white children in the North: reading, writing, arithmetic, and geography. They used textbooks written just for them with names like *The Freedman's Spelling Book.*

Most ex-slave children were very serious about their studies, although sometimes they were mischievous. In one school, the students confused their teacher by trading names or making up new ones every week. One student even called himself Stonewall Jackson, after the famous Confederate general.

But education was clearly very important to the freed children who were lucky enough to attend school. This was proven to one Northern teacher when she asked a group of girls, "What good does it do you to come to school?" One of them replied, "If we are educated, they can't make slaves of us again."

Adapted from an article by James Marten

At schools for freed slaves, such as this one in Vicksburg, Mississippi, children learned how to read and write alongside adults.

STEALING
FREEDOM

ON THE UNDERGROUND RAILROAD

THE UNITED STATES

MINNESOTA

WISCONSIN

Mississippi River

IOWA

Chicago

ILLINOIS

St. Louis

MISSOURI

ARKANSAS

MISSISSIPPI

LOUISIANA

TEXAS

New Orleans

Gulf of Mexico

MEXICO

KEY

☐ free state
☐ slave state
☐ territory (slavery determined individually)
➤ approximate route of flight
● city

SCALE OF MILES

0   100   500 Miles

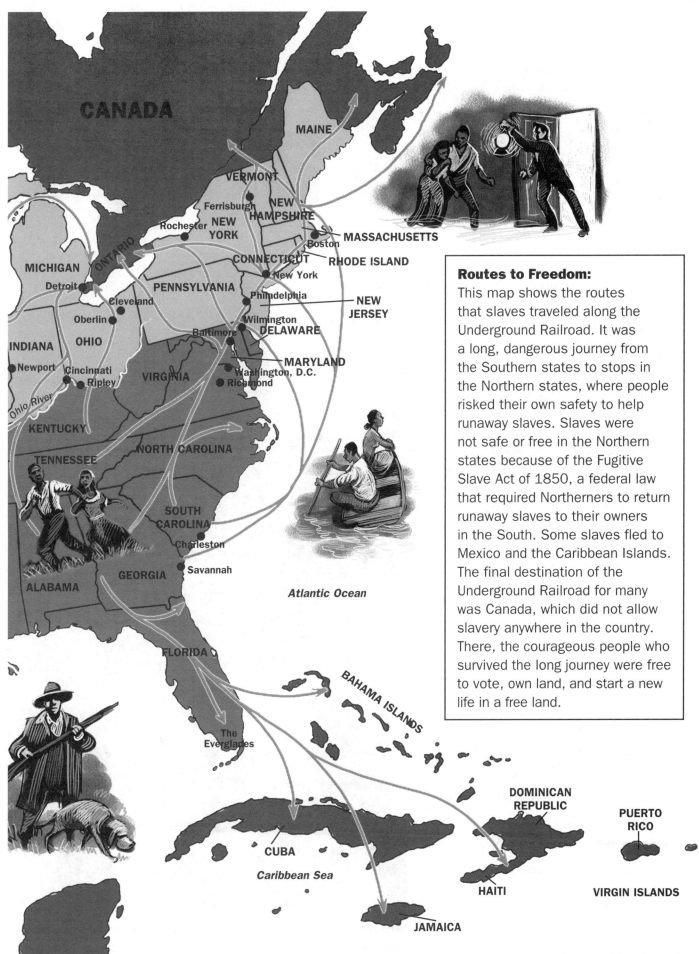

Routes to Freedom:
This map shows the routes that slaves traveled along the Underground Railroad. It was a long, dangerous journey from the Southern states to stops in the Northern states, where people risked their own safety to help runaway slaves. Slaves were not safe or free in the Northern states because of the Fugitive Slave Act of 1850, a federal law that required Northerners to return runaway slaves to their owners in the South. Some slaves fled to Mexico and the Caribbean Islands. The final destination of the Underground Railroad for many was Canada, which did not allow slavery anywhere in the country. There, the courageous people who survived the long journey were free to vote, own land, and start a new life in a free land.

CANADA

MAINE

VERMONT

NEW HAMPSHIRE

Ferrisburgh

Rochester

NEW YORK

MASSACHUSETTS

Boston

CONNECTICUT

RHODE ISLAND

MICHIGAN

ONTARIO

Detroit

Cleveland

New York

PENNSYLVANIA

Philadelphia

NEW JERSEY

Oberlin

Wilmington

DELAWARE

Baltimore

INDIANA

OHIO

MARYLAND

Newport

Cincinnati

Washington, D.C.

VIRGINIA

Richmond

Ripley

Ohio River

KENTUCKY

TENNESSEE

NORTH CAROLINA

SOUTH CAROLINA

Charleston

GEORGIA

Savannah

ALABAMA

Atlantic Ocean

FLORIDA

BAHAMA ISLANDS

The Everglades

DOMINICAN REPUBLIC

PUERTO RICO

CUBA

Caribbean Sea

HAITI

VIRGIN ISLANDS

JAMAICA

Illustrated by Tim Foley

What is Child Labor?

About 246 million children between the ages of 5 and 17 are engaged in "child labor," according to the International Labour Organization's (ILO) 2000 global estimate. An estimated 73 million of these children are below the age of 10.

What is meant by "child labor"? What kind of work constitutes child labor? And where are these child laborers found? How is child labor connected to us as Americans? These are very simple questions. The answers, unfortunately, are not so simple.

It has taken many years to come to some kind of agreement on the definition of child labor. While experts continue to disagree on some aspects of the definition, international human-rights conventions have helped to guide international efforts to eliminate child labor.

In 1989, the UN Convention on the Rights of the Child examined the issue. According to Article 32 of this convention:

"State Parties recognize the right of the child to be protected from economic exploitation and from performing any work that is likely to be hazardous or to interfere with the child's education, or to be harmful to the child's health or physical, mental, spiritual, moral, or social development."

Who picked the cotton that made your jeans? Children in Northern Peru spend hours every day picking cotton, a backbreaking and thorny job.

He's only 14, but he already looks like he's been laboring a long time. His work is crushing rocks to build a road, and he earns less than $1 for a 12-hour workday.

In 2000, the ILO conducted a study of the scope and magnitude of child labor. The Asia-Pacific region has the highest incidence of child labor. About 127.3 million children between the ages of 5 and 14 are found in Asia, 73 million in sub-Saharan Africa, and 17.4 million in Latin American and the Caribbean. And about 5 million are found in both developed countries and transition economies. This is only an estimate; it is nearly impossible to accurately measure the problem. But we know that this problem is widespread.

When people hear the phrase "child labor," they often think of problems in faraway places—problems in poor, developing countries. While it is true that the highest incidence of child labor takes place in these poor countries, America has its share of the problem. In fact, American history is filled with abusive forms of child labor, such as children working in mines, sawmills, and sweatshop factories. Today, some child labor continues to exist in America. We can still find children working on farms under some of the most hazardous conditions. In states such as California and Texas, for example, children are picking onions and other agricultural products that end up in some of our supermarkets and that are eaten by you and me.

Child Labor through the Years

1639 The earliest recorded account of cruelty to a child occurred when a master killed his young apprentice.

1790s Child labor rose in the United States during the Industrial Revolution. Eventually laws were passed to limit how much children can work.

1904 The National Child Labor Committee was formed in the United States.

1909 The first Conference on Children was held at the White House.

1938 The United States Congress passed the Fair Labor Standards Act, freeing children under the age of 16 from having to work.

As Americans, we are also connected to global child labor, directly and indirectly. About 70 percent of child labor takes place in agriculture. This includes the harvesting of bananas in Central America and cocoa beans for chocolate in West Africa and the picking of coffee beans and tea leaves in Latin America and Africa. Some of these agricultural products end up on our supermarket shelves. For better or for worse, we are connected to some of the most unacceptable forms of child labor.

Besides agriculture, what other forms of child labor exist? The list is long, and we can only cite a few categories, to give an idea of the scope of the problem. Some children are used to promote unlawful activities such as the drug trade. Some children are kidnapped and forced to become child soldiers. Others are abducted to perform labor similar to slavery, such as working as servants in other people's homes. Other children, especially those orphaned by HIV/AIDS, are left to fend for themselves on the streets. These are the children who labor from dawn until dusk in dangerous conditions and live without knowing where their next meal will come from.

These 246 million children suffer from some of the cruelest human rights violations on a daily basis.

Adapted from an article by Chivy Sok

Not only are children working rather than going to school, but it is not uncommon in Africa to find children doing dangerous work, such as welding.

Child Labor through the Years

1974 The United States Congress created the Child Abuse Prevention and Treatment Act.

1989 The United Nations adopted the Convention on the Rights of the Child. The convention asks that all member nations protect their children's rights.

1995 Twelve-year-old Craig Kielburger founded Free the Children, an international organization of children who help other children.

2001 The international global movement Say Yes for Children began to gain millions of members worldwide.

2004 The first Children's World Congress on child labor is held in Florence, Italy. A follow-up session is held in India the following year.

2006 As many as 250 million children are being held in bondage and working as slaves around the world.

Education Is Our Hope

The Interact Club of Vashon Island High School has made it possible for some Kenyan orphans to continue their schooling.

Ever since you were five or six years old, the classroom has been an almost daily part of life. There have always been teachers to teach you how to make sense of words on a page, to add and subtract numbers, and to learn the many other skills you will need as an adult.

For millions of children around the world, however, education is still an unfulfilled dream. More than 130 million children between the ages of 6 and 11 are not in school. In most cases, this is due to poverty.

Sometimes children are kept at home because they are needed to do chores, from working on the farm to taking care of younger brothers and sisters. This is especially true for girls, so fewer girls attend school than boys. But for many families, school costs are too high.

While the Convention on the Rights of the Child calls for free primary (elementary) education, many governments cannot afford to cover all educational expenses, so parents must pay school fees and buy books and uniforms. In Kenya, primary school was once free, and almost 90 percent of children attended. But in the 1980s, the government, short on money, started charging. The number of children in school dropped to 50 percent.

AIDS, a disease that has taken the lives of many Africans, makes it especially hard for children to afford the cost of education. The village of Majiwa (ma-GEE-wah) is inhabited by the Luo people, who have long valued education and often pooled their money to send village children to boarding schools to get a better education. AIDS is undoing this custom. Many children have lost parents to AIDS. Without their support, the children cannot afford the cost of school.

Gideon, Carolina, Jacqueline, and Benjamin have lived alone since their mother died in the spring of 2002. The foursome missed weeks of school when they were short on tuition. But they were determined to keep going. Gideon, age 18, aspires to become an engineer, while Benjamin, age 8, says he "likes to read best." To raise money for school fees, Jacqueline and Carolina, ages 10 and 12, collected wood to sell. Still, their chances of staying in school were not good.

But 9,000 miles away in the U.S., on Vashon Island in Washington, a group of high school students was learning about the AIDS epidemic. They were members of a service club called Interact, and they decided they wanted to help.

The students invited Atieno Kombe, who is from Majiwa, to give a presentation at their school. Without an education, children don't have hope or value their lives as much, Atieno told the students who filled the school auditorium. As a result, they get involved in risky behavior, which can lead to AIDS. When children go to school, they have a light shining that keeps them focused, she said.

Afterward, Vashon High School student Rachel Weise said, "We felt bad learning there was a heart and a soul being destroyed by AIDS, but there was also hope. We could help the kids go to school."

The group started fundraising and educating fellow students. They left hundreds of slips of paper with information about AIDS and Africa on desks all over the school and put out collection jars. They quickly raised $1,500, which was used to build a well at the Majiwa high school. Before the well, the children had to collect dirty water from streams, which often made them sick.

The Interact group also decided to pay for Gideon's, Carolina's, Jacqueline's, and Benjamin's school fees. To do this, they hold regular bake sales and sell candy. They especially want to ensure that Jacqueline and Carolina continue their schooling because girls who go to school are half as likely to get AIDS. Education, it turns out, is not only important for developing skills—it is their best hope for life itself.

Young Benjamin has benefited from Interact's fundraising.

"The children are the future . . ."

—Femke Oldham

The banner, which traveled thousands of miles, is held up by Majiwa students.

In fact, educating girls may be the smartest way to bring families out of poverty. Girls who have been to school are more likely to have smaller families, and healthier, better-educated children. The benefits of this education range from being able to read instructions on pill bottles, to making better decisions, to getting a job.

Most countries are committed to making sure all children get some education. Recently, Kenya made primary school free again. Girls who want to go to high school, however, must attend costly boarding schools. On Vashon Island, the bake sales continue; middle school students are selling hacky sacks to help out, too.

Emma Bean shared the dream of her fellow students: "We're hoping that by helping one part of the village, we can help the whole community."

"The children are the future," added Femke Oldham. "We're giving them the opportunity to have a good future with lots of options."

Adapted from an article by Lesley Reed

Hip-Hop at the Museum?

The Smithsonian Institution Opens a New Exhibit with a New Beat

History museums have always looked at the past, but the past isn't always ancient history. Did you know that museums also look at the history being made by young people like you today? The Smithsonian Institution's National Museum of American History recently gathered a broad collection on hip-hop culture for a new exhibit called "Hip-Hop Won't Stop: The Beat, The Rhymes, The Life."

What is Hip-Hop Culture? Hip-hop culture grew out of block parties in New York City, where groups of young people gathered to dance and rap. Today, **hip-hop music** is made of two parts: rapping (MCing) and DJing (production and scratching). **Hip-hop dance** is a freestyle dance that grew from break dancing. **Hip-hop art** is urban-inspired art, like graffiti. Hip-hop culture also includes fashion and street slang.

From the Streets of N.Y. to the World

Important artist movements have always sprung from diverse sources. Hip-hop is a musical art form created by urban black and Latino youth in New York City in the 1970s. Brent D. Glass, director of the National Museum of American History, believes that hip-hop—the music, dance, and art—is now an important part of American culture. The Museum's project traces hip-hop from its beginnings in the 1970s, to its role in America and throughout the world today. Thirty years after it emerged from the inner-city neighborhoods in N.Y., hip-hop has evolved into a fast-moving cultural movement that has spread around the globe.

By collecting memorabilia from artists and producers in the hip-hop community, the museum has created a collection of hip-hop artifacts, from old school rap albums to street fashion. The hip-hop exhibit documents the history and reach of hip-hop, one of the most influential cultural explosions in recent history. "The National Museum of American History is committed to telling the story of the American experience, and with the significant contributions from the hip-hop community, we will be able to place hip-hop in the continuum of American history," he added.

Celebrating Diversity and Creativity

Rap, rhythmically spoken verse over a beat, has roots in rhythm & blues and funk, as well as African, Jamaican, and Latin music. Artists sample music that already exists but assemble it in new ways that haven't been thought of before.

Artists throughout history have looked for ways to comment on society. Rappers, break dancers, and graffiti artists are doing just that. According to the curator of the exhibit, Marvette Pérez, hip-hop began as a way to draw attention to social conditions, like poverty in the inner city. It is an amazingly creative art form that is continually transforming itself. "This music speaks to people across the world as it is easily adapted to the music and language of other countries."

Reaching Out to the Hip-Hop Community

In preparation for "Hip-Hop Won't Stop," the Museum collected objects from all aspects of hip-hop arts and culture—music, technology, sports, graffiti, fashion, break dancing, and language. This includes vinyl records, handwritten lyrics, boom boxes, clothing and costumes, videos and interviews, disc jockey equipment and microphones, and posters and photos.

Over the next several years, the museum plans to reach out to the hip-hop community across the nation to gather additional objects and oral histories—stories of rappers and dancers that will be recorded and saved. During a special ceremony in New York, hip-hop pioneers Russell Simmons, Grandmaster Flash, Afrika Bambaataa, Kool Herc, Ice T, Fab 5 Freddy, and Crazy Legs participated in an event announcing the Museum's plans to build a large collection of hip-hop artifacts. Several of these hip-hop greats, including MC Lyte, were the first to donate objects to "Hip-Hop Won't Stop." A committee made up of artists, producers, and others—the true experts on hip-hop culture—has helped the museum create the exhibit. The long-range vision for "Hip-Hop Won't Stop" includes a large exhibition for millions of museum visitors and a companion traveling display. Check out the Museum's website for more information.

http://americanhistory.si.edu/

Music to Your Ears . . . or Hearing Loss

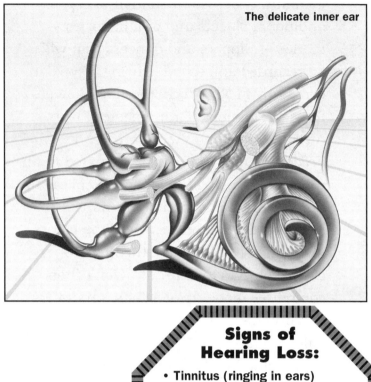

The delicate inner ear

Your ears work hard to keep loud rock music out of your head. It's true. Preventing sound sensation may seem like a peculiar thing for a hearing mechanism to do, but the middle ear does just that.

Thin membranes, tiny bones, irreplaceable hair cells—the intricate structures of the hearing process are extremely delicate. The middle and inner ear are encased in the hardest bone in the body to protect them from most physical bumping and jostling. However, the biggest risk of injury comes from the very thing the ears are designed to handle—sound.

Signs of Hearing Loss:

- Tinnitus (ringing in ears)
- Sounds seem muffled
- Periodic hearing loss
- Difficulty hearing quiet sounds
- Ears feel "full"
- Difficulty separating voices when there is background noise

Warning Signs That Your Music May Be Loud Enough to Damage Your Hearing:

- People complain to you about it. If music is too loud for another person's comfort, it's probably pumping out enough decibels to damage your ears, too;
- When the music stops, you hear ringing or buzzing in your ears; and/or
- You experience some hearing loss for several hours.

Try This!

Cup your hand around the outside of your ear and bend your pinna (outside ear) forward slightly toward the source of a sound. Notice how much louder the sound appears with your hand enlarging the pinna's surface area. The larger the pinna, the more sound is directed into your ear. Old-fashioned ear trumpets acted as enlarged pinnae to help people hear better.

It doesn't have to be rock music, by the way. Any loud music or noise (such as a lawn mower engine) will set two tiny muscles to work pulling the membranes on either side of the middle ear in an effort to stop them from vibrating too wildly. When these muscles grow tired, they become ineffective and the ear is bombarded with too much sound. If a loud enough sound reaches the inner ear often enough, over a long enough period of time, it may cause permanent damage to the hair cells. The louder the sound, the less time it takes for hearing loss to occur . . . at 115 dB, or decibels—the noise from a chainsaw, for example—this can take less than 15 minutes.

Hearing loss results because damaged hair cells cannot fire nerve impulses, so no sound information reaches the brain. While frogs and sharks grow new hair cells throughout life, people don't, so this type of hearing loss is permanent.

Noise-induced hearing loss affects mainly the higher frequency ranges (human voices are usually among the first to go). Hearing aids, which boost all frequencies evenly, are of little help. "Audiologists and hearing specialists will earn a lot of money soon, when the 'rock' generation reaches their sixties!" says Roederer.

So, be kind to your ears—years of good music await!

Adapted from an article by Fiona Bayrock

Hearing "Bells"

Sound intensity (loudness) is measured in units of decibels (dB), the "bels" a shortening of "bells," from Alexander Graham Bell, the inventor of the telephone. The decibel scale usually ranges from 0–140 dB. Any sound above 85 decibels can cause ear damage. Talking softly is about 30 dB. Typical conversation is about 60 dB. But a jet, a boom box, headphones, or a rock concert can be 100 to 140 dB, easily capable of causing permanent hearing loss in minutes or seconds.

What You Can Do to Help Prevent Hearing Loss From Listening to Music:

- Turn down the volume. The quieter, the better—but even a small reduction could make a big difference.
- Take breaks every 10 to 15 minutes to allow your ears to rest.
- Choose room speakers instead of earphones. You may not realize how loud your earphones are, but another person in the room might help to keep the speaker volume at a reasonable level.
- Wear protective earphones or plugs when exposed to loud noises, such as at a concert.
- If you find yourself standing in front of speakers at a concert, move.
- Plug your ears with your fingers when you encounter unexpected loud noise.
- Pay attention to the warning signs. If you experience temporary ringing in your ears or hearing loss after listening to music, change your listening habits to prevent it from happening again. Next time, these effects may be permanent.
- Have your ears tested regularly, so if you are experiencing hearing loss, you can make changes to slow or stop the process.

EGYPT THE GIFT OF THE NILE

Mediterranean Sea

Nile Delta

The Nile River was vitally important to ancient Egyptians. It gave them food, water for their crops, and a waterway along which they could transport their goods. A Greek historian once called Egypt "The Gift of the Nile," because the river allowed the nation to grow and thrive. Without the Nile, ancient Egypt probably would not have become the incredibly rich, cultured civilization it was. The lives—and livelihoods—of ancient Egyptians depended on this great river.

It was more than 7,000 years ago that people first settled along the banks of the Nile and began to grow crops in its fertile floodplains. Centuries later, cities developed beside the river. Near the cities, the pharaohs built pyramids to house their tombs and their riches.

The Nile begins in the south and flows northward to the Mediterranean Sea. Use the map key to locate some of the famous pyramids of ancient Egypt, and see how farmlands follow the river.

Adapted from an article by Ann Jordan
Illustrated by Tim Foley

MEMPHIS

SINAI

EGYPT

Red Sea

Nile River

•THEBES

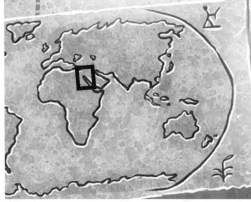

MAP KEY

Some Major Pyramids:

1. **The Step Pyramid of Djoser** at Sakkara, Egypt's first pyramid (around 2630 B.C.)

2. **The Bent Pyramid** at Dashur (around 2600 B.C.)

3. **The Red Pyramid** at Dashur (around 2600 B.C.)

4. **The Great Pyramid Complex** at Giza (around 2500 B.C.)

5. **The Pyramid of Neferirkara** at Abusir (around 2400 B.C.)

Farming Areas

HELP WANTED

If there had been newspapers in ancient Egypt, citizens might have read these job offerings . . .

in Ancient Egypt

NOW HIRING POTTERS

Craftsmen needed to make canopic jars for storage of mummified organs. Must be able to make and decorate jars from pottery, limestone, precious stone, and wood. Please bring samples of your carvings (such as inscriptions and heads of humans, animals, and birds).

SEEKING MUSCLE MEN

Strong men needed to cut stones in rock quarries. Must be able to use chisels, saws, mallets, and hammers. Heavy lifting required.

CAN YOU PLOW?

Farmers needed to grow flax, olives, and barley, as well as taking care of cows, sheep, goats, and pigs. Job involves plowing soil, scattering seeds, and harvesting crops. Families may apply.

WANTED: MEDICAL EXPERTS

Male and female doctors needed. Experience in curing sickness and performing surgery is required. Must be able to prepare and prescribe medicines made from minerals, plants, and animal parts. Knowledge of magic is helpful for cases where all other cures fail.

LOOKING FOR PRIEST

Local temple needs priest or priestess to conduct ceremonies, write sacred texts, and run daily business of temple. Knowledge of stars and constellations necessary to help determine locations for new pyramids.

CAN YOU KEEP CAREFUL RECORDS OF MANY THINGS? CAN YOU WRITE WELL AND MIX GOOD INK? IF SO, THIS JOB IS FOR YOU!

Scribes needed to prepare contracts, write letters, copy texts, and keep records. Only men who have completed scribal training and can prepare their own inks from soot, charcoal, and minerals need apply.

IMMEDIATE OPENINGS FOR EMBALMERS

Now hiring men to mummify the dead. Experience removing body fluids and organs is necessary. Must be able to make bodies look their best for the afterlife.

Adapted from an article by Chris Graf
Illustrated by Ben Hodson

ALL WRAPPED UP
THE MANY TASKS OF MUMMYMAKERS

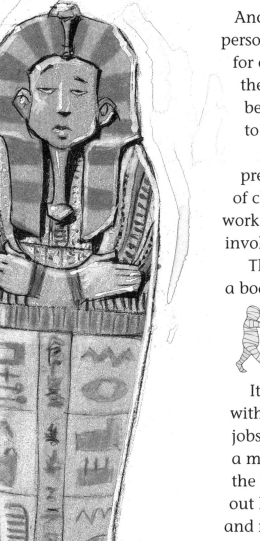

Ancient Egyptians believed that after a person died, he or she lived on in spiritual form for eternity. To help the spirit reconnect with the body in the afterlife, the body had to be preserved. Mummification was a way to prepare the body for the spirit's return.

You probably know that mummies are preserved dead bodies wrapped in strips of cloth. But you might not know how much work and how many different people were involved in making mummies.

The three main processes in mummifying a body were:

- ✔ **removing the internal organs**
- ✔ **drying the body**
- ✔ **protecting the remains**

It took about 70 days to make a mummy, with many different people doing different jobs. Let's take a step-by-step look at making a mummy and find out who was involved in the work. (Count the words in boldface to find out how many different jobs were involved, and remember, there were probably many more we don't know about.)

STEP 1 Someone died. If the dead person was a pharaoh, a special burial chamber—perhaps inside a pyramid—had been built while he or she was alive.

STEP 2 **Embalmers** did the main work of making mummies. Some embalmers worked in special buildings; others worked in tents. After washing the body, the embalmer placed it onto a wooden table. Then he made a long cut on the left side of the body, below the ribs. Through this cut, he removed the liver, lungs, stomach, and intestines. (These were mummified separately.) He used a metal hook to pull the brain out through the nose. The heart was usually left in the body. During this process, **priests** chanted prayers to protect the mummy.

Potters made vases called canopic jars, named after a god. The embalmer placed the mummified organs into four jars. Each jar was decorated with images of a god and prayers were written on the outside to protect the contents.

STEP 3 The embalmers and their assistants covered the body with natron, a saltlike chemical collected by **natron gatherers** along lakeshores. Natron dried the body and prevented bacteria from decaying the body. It could take as long as 40 days for the body to dry completely.

STEP 4

Once the body was dried, it was cleaned and coated with oils, resins, and perfumes to purify it. Sometimes sawdust or linen pads were put inside the body to fill out the shape. Then the embalmer sewed up the cut and placed jewelry and amulets on the body. (Amulets are objects intended to protect against evil.)

Herbalists made and gathered oils, perfumes, resins, and spices from plants growing along the Nile. The embalmers used some of these substances to clean, dry, and perfume the body, and used others to preserve and wrap the skin. **Jewelers** made amulets, necklaces, bracelets, and rings.

STEP 5

Using strips of linen, the embalmers wrapped the fingers, toes, arms, and legs individually. Often the arms were folded across the chest. More layers of linen were wrapped around the body. The embalmer painted a sticky resin between the layers as a waterproof layer to protect the mummy. A scribe wrote the dead person's name on one of the bindings. There might be hundreds of yards of linen covering the body. The wrapping process took about 15 days.

Farmers grew and harvested flax plants for their long, strong fibers. **Weavers** wove these fibers into linen cloth, which was made into rolls of bandages and other cloths. Some linen was also soaked in oils and resins and placed inside the body. **Papermakers** collected wild reeds, or papyrus, growing along the river and made paperlike scrolls. **Scribes** wrote spells from the *Book of the Dead* onto these scrolls.

STEP 6

In some cases a mask was placed over the head. If the dead person was a pharaoh, the mask might be made of gold. The mask was wrapped, then a final cloth covered the entire mummy.

Artists made portrait masks and painted the coffin with images and hieroglyphics.

STEP 7

The mummy was placed into a coffin. Sometimes several coffins were nested inside each other, especially if the person was very important or wealthy. The scrolls were placed in the coffin with the mummy to help him or her in the afterlife.

Sculptors and **carpenters** made coffins as well as artifacts and furniture.

STEP 8

The coffin was brought to the person's home. There, the funeral procession began as family and friends took the coffin to the tomb where the funeral took place. The funeral procession included family, friends, servants, and sometimes professional **mourners** who cried for the dead.

Adapted from an article by Damian Fagan
Illustrated by Kevin Menck

Fun and GAMES in Early America

Just as they are for today's children, games and sports were an important part of the lives of children growing up before 1492. Native American kids—and adults, too—enjoyed a variety of games and sports. But they weren't just pastimes: they also taught life lessons and skills. Games and sports were for everyone: men, women, children, and the elderly. Some games were played by one person, and others were team sports that could include an entire village.

More Than Child's Play

Through play, children learned valuable skills. Many children's games mimicked adult behavior, such as hunting and stalking. Practicing silent footsteps and quiet breathing while sneaking up on someone was fun, and it trained children to be good hunters. (Haven't you had fun sneaking up on a friend or parent?) Wrestling also taught important lessons and built strength and stamina. Good wrestlers have to think, plan, and stay one move ahead of their opponents.

Running games and races were popular. Running was useful for hunting and gathering food and for delivering messages in a hurry. Races were run over short and long distances—up to 25 miles—and often involved obstacles such as trees or rivers. For some races, children had to spin around, then run while dizzy! These runners improved their balance as well as their speed and endurance.

Teamwork and Sportsmanship

Groups of children played many different sports. Team sports included everyone, regardless of their skill level. Teams played to win, but fair play and sportsmanship were just as important as winning. Many games had judges, but individual players were expected to play fairly. Poor sports and cheaters were punished.

Ball games were popular with some groups, who made balls out of carved bone or wood. Sometimes small pieces of animal skins were stitched together and stuffed to make a ball. Most ball games involved hitting or kicking the ball. While sportsmanship was important, games were rough and rules were few. Women and girls often played separately from men and boys.

Early Field Hockey

A popular team sport for women and girls was shinny. Using sticks that looked a bit like modern hockey sticks, the players tried to move a ball down the field to score a goal. Players had to work as a team to be successful. Shinny also could be rough sometimes.

Lacrosse, the "Little War"

In many areas, lacrosse was the most popular sport for men and boys. It was played by two opposing teams. The teams could have any number of players— from a few dozen to a few hundred—as long as each team had the same number. Each player had a stick with a scoop-shaped woven basket at one end. Using these basket-sticks, teammates passed a ball down the field and tried to score a goal. Lacrosse was a physically demanding and intense game. The Cherokee called it "little war." Players were allowed to pull hair, hit each other with their stick, and even wrestle.

Six hundred years ago, kids played tug-of-war and guessing games. They traded with each other and competed for the best prizes. Boys and girls played together and separately, having fun and learning skills they would use when they grew up. Many games we play today—lacrosse, baseball, hockey, and soccer—came from Native American sports. Rough-and-tumble competition, yes. But teamwork and cooperation are an equally important part of the legacy of these first American games.

Adapted from an article by Kelsie Ingham
Illustrated by David Kooharian

GETTING WELL:

Healing the Sick in Early America

Do you go to the doctor when you are sick? Hundreds of years ago, a Native American child who was sick was also cared for by people whose specialty was healing. Some of these specialists were herbalists, people who knew all about healing with medicines made from plants and animals. Some were spiritual leaders, who might have worn ceremonial masks to put on the power of a healing spirit. With music and chants, the spiritual leader would comfort the sick child and invite healing power to enter the house. Depending on how sick the patient was, the "house call" might last several days and include special ceremonies.

These healers were highly respected by all members of the tribe—some had almost as much power as the chief did.

Healers were guided by the spirits to choose the correct medicines, songs, rituals, and chants to heal. Their medicines came from the land around them: leaves, tree bark, roots, and herbs. Medicine made from the bark of a certain willow tree was used by some Indians to stop pain. (The willow has a chemical similar to what is used in making aspirin.) The Iroquois boiled the roots of a geranium flower to make a tea that helped dry wounds and sores. The roots of the yellow lady's slipper flower were used by the Cherokee to treat colds.

Healers also had other ways to treat sickness. They often performed healing rituals in sweat lodges. These special lodges were very hot inside, causing the sick patients to sweat away their illness. In the Southwest, the Navajo healers created pictures with colored sand near a sick person. The sand absorbed the evil that was causing the sickness, then blew away in the wind, taking the sickness with it.

From willow bark to aspirin, from sweat lodges to warm baths—have things really changed in the last 500 years? No matter when you grow up, you still need to "see the doctor" when you get sick.

Adapted from an article by Barbara Hagen
Illustrated by Lois Beardslee

aandag begoosinh = crow's mint

The leaves taste like oregano and were made into tea, to help cure stomach and intestinal problems.

manaboozhoo obiikwazh = yellow lily bulb

A paste made from the bulb of this wild lily drew poison from insect and snake bites.

ozaawaadzhibik = golden thread

A tea from this root was used to soothe sore throats.

53

NAVAJO CODE TALKERS

Bullets and shells tore through the air as U.S. Marines hit the beach. On the sands of Iwo Jima island, any other World War II cryptograph or code machine would have been too slow to use in the heat of battle. But the Marines had highly mobile cryptographs, each with two arms, two legs, and an unbreakable code.

From the first day's invasion to the final battle a month later, the human code machines, Navajo Soldiers, kept messages crackling over military radios. *Gini,* the code said. *Behnaalitsosie. Neasjah. Lotso.* Throughout the dangerous combat, more mysterious words filled the airwaves. Finally, as a photographer took the famous picture of the American flag flying over Mt. Suribachi, the news went out in Navajo.

Naastosi Thanzie Dibeh Shida Dahnestsa Tkin Shush Wollachee Moasi Lin Achi.

Ordinary Marines listening to this babble were as baffled as Japanese soldiers intercepting the messages. Had they spoken Navajo, they would have recognized the words — "Mouse Turkey Sheep Uncle Ram Ice Bear Ant Cat Horse Intestines."

But what could such nonsense mean? To the Navajo Code Talkers, the first letter of each word spelled out Mt. Suribachi. Other code filled in the announcement: Iwo Jima was under American control.

The Navajo Code Talkers were unique in code history. From 1942 to 1945, more than 400 Code Talkers stormed the beaches of Pacific islands. Instantly encoding and decoding messages, they helped Marines win the war in the Pacific. Even today, their code remains one of the few in history that was never broken.

In Navajo, Memory Is Everything

When World War II began, hundreds of Navajo men volunteered to fight. Most had never been off their reservation, a high, barren plain stretching across Arizona, Utah, and New Mexico. There they lived as a separate nation, as many still do today. The reservation had no electricity or indoor plumbing, and only a few schools. Most Navajo herded sheep and bought from government trading posts what little they needed and could not make. They spoke some English, but the business of their daily lives was conducted in their own language.

Among languages that were spoken by only tens of thousands of Americans, Navajo was the language least likely to be known to foreigners. The language was entirely oral. Not a single book had ever been written in Navajo.

Unlike English, Navajo is a tonal language. Its vowels rise and fall depending on the situation. Change the pitch or accent of a Navajo word and you change its meaning. Each Navajo verb contains its own subjects, objects, and adverbs. A single verb can

Navajo Indians' graves in Window Rock, Arizona

translate into an entire sentence. In Navajo, one speaker said, words "paint a picture in your mind."

The Navajo code was proposed by a non-Navajo, Philip Johnston. The son of a missionary father, Johnson had spent his childhood living among the Navajo and spoke their language fluently. Marine officers were skeptical at first. American armies had used other Indian languages to send messages during World War I. Yet because the ancient dialects had no words for machine gun or tank, the experiment failed. Johnston had a better idea — a language combined with a code.

At Camp Elliott, north of San Diego, California, Johnston arranged a test. "Translate some messages from Navajo to English and back again," he told some old friends. As iron-jawed Marines listened in, their faces went slack. The words were not encoded, yet top cryptographers had no hope of deciphering them. Navajo itself was a mystery, even without a code. Soon, the Marines went looking for what they now call "a few good men," fluent in English and Navajo.

Making a Code

The Navajo language contained no words for the horrors of war. Bomber, battleship, grenade — all were terms foreign to the Navajo. But in making their code, the Navajo soldiers rooted it, like their lives, in nature. They named military planes after birds. *Gini*, Navajo for "chicken hawk," became "dive bomber." *Neasjah*, meaning "owl," meant "observation plane." They named ships after fish. *Lotso*, meaning "whale," was the code word for "battleship," and *beshlo* — "iron fish" — meant "submarine."

To spell out proper names, the Code Talkers encoded a Navajo zoo. Marines spell out abbreviations with their own alphabet, which begins Able, Baker, Charlie . . . The Navajo version began *Wollachee*, *Shush*, *Moasi*, meaning Ant, Bear, Cat.

Finally, Code Talkers created clever terms for friends and enemies. Lieutenant was translated as "One Silver Bar." Mussolini, Italy's fascist dictator, was *Adee-yaats-iin-Tsoh* — "Big Gourd Chin." Hitler became *Daghailchiih* — "Moustache Smeller."

Test Time

With just 400 words encoded, the Navajo put their code to the test. They handed a message to Navy intelligence officers, who spent three weeks trying and failing to decipher it. Then, armed with a code and M-1 rifles, a few dozen Code Talkers shipped out to the Pacific. Two more remained behind to teach the code to other Navajo recruits.

The code talkers had to memorize the entire vocabulary of 411 terms. In code competitions with non-Navajo marines, the Navajo code talkers always won in both speed and accuracy. Even the most complicated reports and instructions were transmitted without a single error — an achievement that regular communications men speaking in code were unable to duplicate. The code was so successful that the Japanese and Germans failed to decipher a single syllable of the thousands of messages sent with it.

Fourth Marine Division Code Talkers on the island of Maui, Hawaiian Islands, in 1945, shortly after their return from the invasion of Iwo Jima

After the war, some of the code talkers went to work for the Bureau of Indian Affairs. Others found work as interpreters, engineers, and construction supervisors. Still others continued their education and became teachers, lawyers, and doctors.

Navajo code remained a secret until 1965. In March 1989, the surviving code talkers were reunited in Phoenix, Arizona, and honored by the commandant of the Marine Corps. A statue was unveiled at the ceremony. In a language that needs no decoding, Marine major Howard Conner assessed their contribution. "Without the Navajos," Conner said, "the Marines would never have taken Iwo Jima."

Adapted from an article by Bruce Watson

Viva La Causa

Chavez's Fight for Social Justice

Imagine it is the 1930s, and you are a Mexican American child. Your migrant labor family travels from farm to farm harvesting whatever crop is in season—strawberries, lettuce, peas, string beans, grapes, apples. The roof over your head at night could be the old family car, a tent, or a one-room shack. You have no electricity or running water. After working a long day, your parents are tired and sore from bending and planting, weeding, or picking crops. You dread going to yet another school where you might be laughed at because your shoes are worn out, and you cannot speak English well.

In the 1930s and 1940s, agricultural workers toiled under tough conditions like those described here. Migrant laborers were the most poorly paid, housed, fed, and educated workers in America. In addition, there often was no water to drink in the fields. Old and heavy tools made the farming jobs more backbreaking and exhausting. Pesticides used on the crops endangered the workers' health.

Unfortunately, much of that still is true today for migrant workers in America. But some changes have been made, mostly through the work of Cesar E. Chavez. In the 1950s, Chavez was a migrant worker in the fields around San Jose, California. He spent his evenings planning house meetings for the Community Service Organization (CSO), which was trying to unify and empower poor people through the strength of their votes.

Chavez helped migrant workers find housing, medical care, food, and legal aid, but he wanted more for them. He knew that the biggest problem they faced was the Bracero Program. Braceros—Mexicans with U.S. government permission to work as laborers in America—earned less money and were willing to live in worse conditions than the migrant Mexican American workers. The presence of braceros caused migrant laborers to lose jobs or forced them to work for even less pay.

Chavez was aware of the peaceful teachings of India's Mohandas "Mahatma" Gandhi and America's Rev. Dr. Martin Luther King, Jr. He believed that change could be achieved through nonviolence. So in 1959, with ten thousand marchers, he staged a **sit-in** at a ranch that hired braceros. The negative publicity from the television coverage forced the farmer to stop employing braceros. Chavez then decided to commit all of his time to organizing a **union** of farm

Chavez marches in a picket line to support a boycott of grapes.

workers, despite the fact that others before him had tried to do the same and failed.

Chavez, Dolores Huerta, and other **activists** who believed in La Causa ("The Cause"), as his movement was called, traveled from farm to farm. They talked to workers about health and safety issues, wages, and the need to form a

A **sit-in** is a demonstration in which participants seat themselves in a place related to the cause and refuse to move.

A **union** is a group of employees who join together to improve their working conditions.

Activists are people of action, such as demonstrations or strikes, who promote or oppose people or ideas.

A mural in San Francisco, California, reminds Mexican immigrants to demand fair treatment for hard work.

union. It was difficult because the laborers often moved from job to job. But Chavez was patient: "When you organize, you must dig it bit by bit, very deliberately and carefully. It's like digging a ditch. You take one shovelful at a time," he said.

On September 30, 1962, the first convention of Chavez's National Farm Workers Association (NFWA) was held in Fresno, California. Three years later, the still-young, but growing, union voted to join Filipino farm workers in a **strike** against local Delano (a city in south-central California) grape growers. Union members agreed not to pick any grapes until the Filipino workers got better pay and working conditions.

When the **vineyards** hired other workers to pick the grapes, NFWA members marched near the grape fields carrying signs that said "*Huelga!*"— Spanish for "strike." Chavez convinced the

A **strike** occurs when employees refuse to work, and the business owner is left without a labor force.

Vineyards are areas of ground planted with grapevines.

Fasts are acts of abstaining from eating food.

A **boycott** is an expression of protest by refraining from buying or using an item.

new workers to stop picking. Soon, grapes were rotting on the vines. But the owners still refused to agree to the workers' requests.

In an attempt to bring more attention to the strike and La Causa, Chavez organized a three-hundred-mile march from Delano to Sacramento, California, in the spring of 1966. Television cameras were there once again, broadcasting the event on the news. During the march, Chavez received word that one of the vineyards was ready to negotiate with the NFWA.

In addition to sit-ins, strikes, and marches, Chavez used other nonviolent methods to bring about change. He spoke to religious leaders and university students about social justice, gained their support, and raised money for La Causa. He went on several *fasts.* And Chavez announced a nationwide **boycott** of California grapes as a way to get other vineyard owners to change their conditions and pay

scales, too. It ultimately became the most effective strategy and gained nationwide attention and support.

Throughout the 1970s and 1980s, Chavez peacefully, but forcefully, tried to keep the migrant workers organized and united and demanding change. His efforts made a huge impact on farm workers throughout the United States. But his hard work and fasting took its toll on his health. When Chavez died in 1993, thousands of people came to pay their respects to this hero of migrant farm workers and Mexican Americans.

Adapted from an article by Diane L. Brooks

"He Inspired Others":
An Interview with Cesar's Grandson

Why should young people know about Cesar E. Chavez?

Fernando Chavez, a 13-year-old grandson of Cesar E. Chavez, responded, "Children should know what my grandfather did so they will be inspired to help others. My Tata (grandfather) helped lots of families. Just as others gave food to help his family, my grandfather gave away food and clothing to help others. He talked to people about what to do so they could help themselves. I hope that I, too, can help those in need. When I see families living in campers and trucks, I feel so sad. I hope that migrant families can live a normal life, in a normal house."

What do you remember about your grandfather?

"I had a birthday, then just three days after, Grandfather died. Many, many people came to pray and give final thanks for all that he had done for them. My dad reminds me that on that day, I took my sandwich and went to eat it by his graveside; my last moments with Tata. My family and I really miss him, especially at Christmastime. Tata loved being with his (33) grandchildren.

"My grandfather also loved his dogs. He had two German shepherds, guard dogs, called Huelga (the Spanish word for 'strike') and Boycott, and later, another named Oso (the Spanish word for 'bear'). They are buried near him."

Fernando Chavez

About Fernando Chavez
Fernando Chavez turned 13 years old in 2001. With his two brothers and one sister, he lives with his family in La Paz, a small community near Bakersfield, California. His father, Paul F. Chavez, was the sixth of the eight children of Cesar and Helen Chavez.

What stories do you remember about Cesar E. Chavez?

"I remember stories about my grandfather's courage and bravery. He gave a lot of speeches, and he helped a lot of people. There were stories about hard work in the fields, and terrible things like farmers with guns, people trying to tear the Union apart, and racism—people yelling names. I'm grateful that I don't have to go through that. These stories make me want to stand up and do something when I am older and braver. I will stand up! But I have also learned from my grandfather that the best way to solve a problem is to talk it out. These stories mean a lot to me, and I'm inspired to help those who go through tough times. And there are still problems—people with no place to live, boycotts, and problems with contracts between farmers and workers."

What is it like to be the grandson of a famous person, and the son of a father who continues to work for "the cause"?

"It feels good, and I'm proud that my grandfather is in history books. But it puts a lot of pressure on me—I can't put a bad name on my grandfather or my family. I know that I need to stay under control."

Fernando, his father, and his brothers

Adapted from an article by Diane L. Brooks

The Petticoat Vote

"A thousand kisses." That's how Elizabeth Cady Stanton ended letters to her children. And seven children meant a lot of kisses! Like other young mothers in the 1800s, Elizabeth cooked, cleaned, and sewed for her family. And through it all, she fought for the rights of women.

American women didn't always have the same rights as men. Married women couldn't own property, and no woman could vote. Elizabeth didn't think that was fair. So in 1848, she organized a meeting in Seneca Falls, New York, and suggested that women should have the right to vote. America was shocked. Most Americans—even most women—thought women should stick to wearing petticoats (frilly underskirts) and leave politics to men.

Elizabeth had big ideas, but how could she change America's thinking when she had a family to care for? Her husband was often away from home. She couldn't leave her children alone while she traveled around the country arguing for the right to vote. Then Elizabeth Cady Stanton met Susan B. Anthony. Susan was working to outlaw slavery and alcohol abuse, and fighting for men and women to be paid the same wages. Elizabeth's ideas about woman suffrage—

Women were expected to spend a lot of time in the kitchen (below).

the right to vote—made sense to Susan. The two women became a team. Elizabeth stayed home, organized meetings, and wrote letters and speeches. Susan, who had no husband or children, traveled across America giving Elizabeth's speeches. Elizabeth said about Susan: "I forged the thunderbolts, she fired them."

By 1867, Elizabeth's children were old enough that she could leave them. For the next ten years, she traveled eight months each year, giving speeches, meeting with lawmakers, and building support all over America. But it wasn't until 1920—18 years after Elizabeth Cady Stanton's death—that her dream came true. The 19th Amendment gave American women the right to vote in all elections.

Susan B. Anthony might sit on the face of our dollar coin, but it was her friend, Elizabeth Cady Stanton, who first inspired women to fight for the right to vote. That busy mother with the sparkling eyes and kind smile worked tirelessly over her lifetime for what she believed was fair. A thousand kisses to you, Elizabeth Cady Stanton!

Adapted from an article by Carol Peterson

Elizabeth Cady Stanton   **Susan B. Anthony**

Instead, they organized meetings and made speeches to give women more choices (below right).

The Changing Face

Many Americans take for granted their right to vote. Today, seven out of every ten Americans are allowed to vote. (The rest are not yet old enough.)

1787

The Constitution of the United States creates the federal (national) government. The Constitution leaves all decisions about voting to the individual states. Most states decide to allow only white, property-owning men over the age of 21 to vote.

At the same time, many people believe that property owners have a stronger interest in government. Women, African Americans, and poor people are not allowed to vote.

1821

New York State drops the property-owning requirement for white males. Soon, other states do the same.

1870

The Constitution is amended, or changed, to give African American men the right to vote. This change is the 15th Amendment.

# of American Voters

But it hasn't always been this way.

Check out this timeline. It shows important changes in the history of American voting.

1920

Again, the Constitution is amended—this time to give women the right to vote. This is the 19th Amendment.

1965

Congress passes the Voting Rights Act of 1965. This law says that the unfair voting practices in many states, which make it difficult or impossible for African Americans to vote, are illegal and have to stop.

1971

The 26th Amendment to the Constitution lowers the voting age from 21 to 18. This happens because young American soldiers are dying in a war in Vietnam. Many people believe it is unfair that young men under 21 can be sent to fight and die in a war but are not allowed to vote.

Today

With few exceptions, every American citizen 18 years old or older is allowed to vote. The exceptions vary from state to state. For example, some states do not allow people to vote if they have committed serious crimes or are mentally incompetent.

Adapted from an article by Mike Weinstein

A Long, Hard MARCH

> ## *"Every American citizen must have an equal right to vote."*
>
> ### President Lyndon B. Johnson, March 15, 1965
>
> Today, every time an African American citizen votes in an election, Joanne Bland and Lynda Lowery have a reason to smile. In a large part it's thanks to them and the many thousands of other people who marched for equal voting rights in the 1960s that African Americans can vote freely today.
>
> Joanne and Lynda are sisters from Selma, Alabama. When they were young girls, African Americans living in the South were frequently prevented from voting. They were beaten, forced to take difficult tests, and made to pay fees when they tried to vote. This violated the 15th Amendment to the Constitution, which states that a person cannot be

Often, police officers enforced unfair voting practices.

The Selma marchers on their way to Montgomery

As used here, a **march** is an organized public walk by a group of people for a specific cause or issue. Often, marchers are protesting something they believe is unfair. When they arrive at their destination, marchers often continue their protest with speeches, chants, and songs.

denied the right to vote because of the color of his or her skin. During the 1960s, many Americans protested the violation of African Americans' rights.

On March 7, 1965, 15-year-old Lynda and 11-year-old Joanne began to **march** with 600 people to Alabama's capital city of Montgomery. After only six blocks, they were attacked by 200 police officers with tear gas and nightsticks. (Tear gas irritates the eyes and nose and makes people cough. Nightsticks are wooden clubs sometimes used by police officers.)

Lynda remembers how the tear gas caused blinding tears and burned her nose. She panicked. She was running for safety when a police officer grabbed her and hit her in the face and head with his nightstick. Somehow, she managed to find Joanne and get to safety. Later, she needed 24 stitches to sew up her wounds. That terrible day became known as Bloody Sunday.

Just a few weeks later, on March 21, more than 3,000 people set out from Selma to march to Montgomery. People had come from all over the country to take part in the march. This time, the marchers were protected by military police. Joanne participated in that march, and Lynda walked the entire 54 miles to Montgomery. She and the other marchers walked 12 miles a day—sometimes in the rain—and slept in tents at night.

By the time they reached Montgomery five days later, 25,000 people had joined the march for equal voting rights for African Americans. They were met by Dr. Martin Luther King, Jr., a powerful civil rights leader and Baptist minister.

When Lynda reached Montgomery, she felt that she had really accomplished something. She had feared for her safety throughout the march, but she kept going. Five months later, Congress passed the Voting Rights Act of 1965. It prohibits all unfair voting practices due to race and color.

Joanne has kept memories of the march alive by becoming the director and one of the founders of the Voting Rights Museum in Selma. She says that the purpose of the museum is "to teach the younger generation the awesome things that ordinary people can do."

Adapted from an article by Chris Graf

Dr. Martin Luther King Jr. speaking to the crowds in Montgomery